CCNA Self-Study
CCNA Portable
Command Guide

Scott Empson

Cisco Press

800 East 96th Street
Indianapolis, IN 46240 USA

CCNA Self-Study
CCNA Portable Command Guide

Scott Empson

Copyright© 2006 Cisco Systems, Inc.

Cisco Press logo is a trademark of Cisco Systems, Inc.

Published by:
Cisco Press
800 East 96th Street
Indianapolis, IN 46240 USA

Printed in the United States of America 1 2 3 4 5 6 7 8 9 0

First Printing   November 2005

Library of Congress Cataloging-in-Publication Number: 2005930384

ISBN: 1-58720-158-5

Warning and Disclaimer

This book is designed to provide information about the Certified Cisco Networking Associate (CCNA) exam and the commands needed at this level of network administration. Every effort has been made to make this book as complete and as accurate as possible, but no warranty or fitness is implied.

The information is provided on an "as is" basis. The authors, Cisco Press, and Cisco Systems, Inc. shall have neither liability nor responsibility to any person or entity with respect to any loss or damages arising from the information contained in this book or from the use of the discs or programs that may accompany it.

The opinions expressed in this book belong to the author and are not necessarily those of Cisco Systems, Inc.

Trademark Acknowledgments

All terms mentioned in this book that are known to be trademarks or service marks have been appropriately capitalized. Cisco Press or Cisco Systems, Inc. cannot attest to the accuracy of this information. Use of a term in this book should not be regarded as affecting the validity of any trademark or service mark.

Feedback Information

At Cisco Press, our goal is to create in-depth technical books of the highest quality and value. Each book is crafted with care and precision, undergoing rigorous development that involves the unique expertise of members from the professional technical community.

Readers' feedback is a natural continuation of this process. If you have any comments regarding how we could improve the quality of this book, or otherwise alter it to better suit your needs, you can contact us through email at feedback@ciscopress.com. Please make sure to include the book title and ISBN in your message.

We greatly appreciate your assistance.

Publisher	John Wait
Editor-in-Chief	John Kane
Executive Editor	Mary Beth Ray
Cisco Representative	Anthony Wolfenden
Cisco Press Program Manager	Jeff Brady
Production Manager	Patrick Kanouse
Senior Development Editor	Christopher Cleveland
Technical Editors	Steve Kalman, Gerlinde Brady, David Kotfila
Editorial Assistant	Raina Han
Book and Cover Designer	Louisa Adair
Composition	Mark Shirar

CISCO SYSTEMS

Corporate Headquarters
Cisco Systems, Inc.
170 West Tasman Drive
San Jose, CA 95134-1706
USA
www.cisco.com
Tel: 408 526-4000
    800 553-NETS (6387)
Fax: 408 526-4100

European Headquarters
Cisco Systems International BV
Haarlerbergpark
Haarlerbergweg 13-19
1101 CH Amsterdam
The Netherlands
www-europe.cisco.com
Tel: 31 0 20 357 1000
Fax: 31 0 20 357 1100

Americas Headquarters
Cisco Systems, Inc.
170 West Tasman Drive
San Jose, CA 95134-1706
USA
www.cisco.com
Tel: 408 526-7660
Fax: 408 527-0883

Asia Pacific Headquarters
Cisco Systems, Inc.
Capital Tower
168 Robinson Road
#22-01 to #29-01
Singapore 068912
www.cisco.com
Tel: +65 6317 7777
Fax: +65 6317 7799

Cisco Systems has more than 200 offices in the following countries and regions. Addresses, phone numbers, and fax numbers are listed on the
Cisco.com Web site at www.cisco.com/go/offices.

Argentina • Australia • Austria • Belgium • Brazil • Bulgaria • Canada • Chile • China PRC • Colombia • Costa Rica • Croatia • Czech Republic
Denmark • Dubai, UAE • Finland • France • Germany • Greece • Hong Kong SAR • Hungary • India • Indonesia • Ireland • Israel • Italy
Japan • Korea • Luxembourg • Malaysia • Mexico • The Netherlands • New Zealand • Norway • Peru • Philippines • Poland • Portugal
Puerto Rico • Romania • Russia • Saudi Arabia • Scotland • Singapore • Slovakia • Slovenia • South Africa • Spain • Sweden
Switzerland • Taiwan • Thailand • Turkey • Ukraine • United Kingdom • United States • Venezuela • Vietnam • Zimbabwe

About the Author

Scott Empson is currently an instructor in the Department of Telecommunications at the Northern Alberta Institute of Technology in Edmonton, Alberta, Canada, where he teaches Cisco routing, switching, and network design courses in a variety of different programs—certificate, diploma, and applied degree—at the post-secondary level. Scott is also the program coordinator of the Cisco Networking Academy Program at NAIT, a Regional Academy covering Central and Northern Alberta. He has earned three undergraduate degrees: a bachelor of arts, with a major in English; a bachelor of education, again with a major in English/Language Arts; and a Bachelor of applied information systems technology, with a major in network management. He currently holds several industry certifications, including CCNP, CCDA, CCAI, and Network+. Prior to instructing at NAIT, he was a junior/senior high school English/language arts/computer science teacher at different schools throughout northern Alberta. Upon completion of this project he plans to complete a master's degree. Scott lives in Edmonton, Alberta, with his wife and two children.

About the Technical Reviewers

Stephen Kalman is a data security trainer. He is the author or tech editor of more than 20 books, courses, and CBT titles. His most recent book is Web Security Field Guide, published by Cisco Press. In addition to those responsibilities he runs a consulting company, Esquire Micro Consultants, that specializes in network security assessments and forensics. Mr. Kalman holds CISSP, CEH, CHFI, CCNA, CCSA (Checkpoint), A+, Network+ and Security+ certifications and is a member of the New York State Bar.

Gerlinde Brady, M.A., CCNP, has been a certified Cisco Systems instructor since 2000. She holds a M.A. degree in education from the University of Hannover, Germany. Besides A+ certification courses and general IT courses, she has been teaching Cisco CCNA and CCNP courses at Cabrillo College since 1999. Her industry experience includes LAN design, network administration, and technical support.

David Kotfila is the director of the Cisco Networking Academy Program at Rensselaer Polytechnic Institute (RPI) in Troy, New York. He is also on the National Advisory Council for the Networking Academy. In the past three years, more than 260 students have received their CCNA and 80 students their CCNP at RPI. Previously, David was the senior manager in charge of training at PSINet, a Tier 1, global, Internet service provider. David enjoys spending time with his family, hiking in the mountains, and kayaking.

Dedications

To Trina, Zach, and Shae. What more can I say but I love you all, and that I promise to turn off the computer now and come outside and play.

Acknowledgments

Once again, this book was not just me; many people were involved:

To the team at Cisco Press: You have again shown me that you are all the best at what you do. Mary Beth, Chris, Patrick, Raina, and John—thank you for your belief in me and my abilities; without you I would still be in my classroom, wondering why this book hasn't been written yet.

To my technical reviewers, Gerlinde, David, and Steve: Thank you for once again keeping me on the straight and narrow and not letting me drift off into the realm of the cloudy and confusing.

Finally, a big thank you goes to Hans Roth, a fellow Cisco Networking Academy instructor at Red River College in Winnipeg, Manitoba. Hans once again helped me out immensely—diagramming my ideas, being the sounding board for my ideas, telling me what worked and what needed to be improved, and best of all, teaching me to juggle at various conferences around North America over the last two years to help reduce the stress of meeting writing deadlines. You are a true friend, Hans, and I can never repay what you have done for me.

This Book Is Safari Enabled

The Safari® Enabled icon on the cover of your favorite technology book means the book is available through Safari Bookshelf. When you buy this book, you get free access to the online edition for 45 days.

Safari Bookshelf is an electronic reference library that lets you easily search thousands of technical books, find code samples, download chapters, and access technical information whenever and wherever you need it.

To gain 45-day Safari Enabled access to this book:

- Go to http://www.ciscopress.com/safarienabled

- Enter the ISBN of this book (shown on the back cover, above the bar code)

- Log in or Sign up (site membership is required to register your book)

- Enter the coupon code
  V2L8-R1YN-MR1Y-YYNY-K4FC

If you have difficulty registering on Safari Bookshelf or accessing the online edition, please e-mail customer-service@safaribooksonline.com.

Contents at a Glance

Introduction   xx

Part I   TCP/IP   1

Chapter 1   How to Subnet   3

Chapter 2   VLSM   21

Chapter 3   Route Summarization   29

Part II   Introduction to Cisco Devices   35

Chapter 4   Cables and Connections   37

Chapter 5   The Command-Line Interface   43

Part III   Configuring a Router   49

Chapter 6   Configuring a Single Cisco Router   51

Part IV   Routing   65

Chapter 7   Static Routing   67

Chapter 8   RIP   73

Chapter 9   IGRP   79

Chapter 10   EIGRP   81

Chapter 11   Single-Area OSPF   87

Part V   Switches   97

Chapter 12   Configuring a Switch   99

Chapter 13   Spanning Tree Protocol and EtherChannel   111

Chapter 14   VLANs   115

Chapter 15   VTP and Inter-VLAN Communication   125

Part VI   Network Administration and Troubleshooting   141

Chapter 16   Backing Up and Restoring Cisco IOS Software and Configurations   143

Chapter 17   Password Recovery Procedures and the Configuration Register   157

Chapter 18 CDP 167

Chapter 19 Telnet 169

Chapter 20 ping and traceroute 173

Chapter 21 SNMP and Syslog 177

Chapter 22 Basic Troubleshooting 179

Part VII Managing IP Services 185

Chapter 23 NAT 187

Chapter 24 DHCP 197

Part VIII Wide-Area Networks 203

Chapter 25 HDLC and PPP 205

Chapter 26 ISDN and DDR 211

Chapter 27 Frame Relay 223

Part IX Network Security 233

Chapter 28 IP Access Control List Security 235

Part X Appendixes 247

Appendix A Complete Configuration Example 249

Appendix B Binary/Hex/Decimal Conversion Chart 265

Appendix C Create Your Own Journal Here 275

Contents

Introduction   xx

Part I   TCP/IP   1

Chapter 1   How to Subnet   3

Class A–E Addresses   3
Converting Between Decimal Numbers and Binary   4
Subnetting a Class C Network Using Binary   4
Subnetting a Class B Network Using Binary   8
Binary ANDing   12
  Question 1   12
  Answer   12
  Question 2   13
  Answer   13
  So Why AND?   14
    Question 3   14
    Answer   14
  Shortcuts in Binary ANDing   15
    Question 4   15
    Answer   15
    Proof   15
    Question 5   16
    Answer   16
    Question 6   16
    Answer   16
The Enhanced Bob Maneuver for Subnetting   16

Chapter 2   VLSM   21

IP Subnet Zero   21
VLSM Example   22
  Step 1 Determine How Many H Bits Will Be Needed to
    Satisfy the Largest Network   23
  Step 2 Pick a Subnet for the Largest Network to Use   23
  Step 3 Pick the Next Largest Network to Work With   24
  Step 4 Pick the Third Largest Network to Work With   25
  Step 5 Determine Network Numbers for Serial Links   27

Chapter 3   Route Summarization   29

Example for Understanding Route Summarization   29
  Step 1: Summarize Winnipeg's Routes   30
  Step 2: Summarize Calgary's Routes   31

Step 3: Summarize Edmonton's Routes   31
Step 4: Summarize Vancouver's Routes   32
Route Summarization and Route Flapping   34
Requirements for Route Summarization   34

Part II   Introduction to Cisco Devices   35

Chapter 4   Cables and Connections   37
Connecting a Rollover Cable to Your Router or Switch   37
Terminal Settings   37
LAN Connections   38
Serial Cable Types   39
Which Cable to Use?   40
568A Versus 568B Cables   42

Chapter 5   The Command-Line Interface   43
Shortcuts for Entering Commands   43
Using the Tab⇄ Key to Complete Commands   43
Using the Question Mark for Help   43
enable Command   44
exit Command   44
disable Command   45
logout Command   45
Setup Mode   45
Keyboard Help   45
History Commands   46
show Commands   47

Part III   Configuring a Router   49

Chapter 6   Configuring a Single Cisco Router   51
Router Modes   51
Global Configuration Mode   52
Configuring a Router Name   52
Configuring Passwords   52
Password Encryption   53
show Commands   53
Interface Names   54
Moving Between Interfaces   57
Configuring a Serial Interface   57
Configuring an Ethernet/Fast Ethernet Interface   57
Creating an MOTD Banner   58
Setting the Clock Time Zone   58
Assigning a Local Host Name to an IP Address   58
no ip domain-lookup Command   59
logging synchronous Command   59

exec-timeout Command   60
Saving Configurations   60
Erasing Configurations   60
Configuration Example: Basic Router Configuration   60

Part IV   Routing   65

Chapter 7   Static Routing   67

Static Routing   67
   The permanent Keyword (Optional)   68
   Static Routes and Administrative Distance (Optional)   68
Default Routing   69
Verifying Static Routes   69
Configuration Example: Static Routes   70

Chapter 8   RIP   73

IP Classless   73
RIP Routing: Mandatory Commands   73
RIP Routing: Optional Commands   74
RIP Version 2   75
Troubleshooting RIP Issues   75
RIP Version 2: Mandatory Commands   76
RIP Version 2: Optional Commands   76
Configuration Example: RIP-2 Routing   76

Chapter 9   IGRP   79

IGRP Routing: Mandatory Commands   79
IGRP Routing: Optional Commands   80
Troubleshooting IGRP Issues   80

Chapter 10   EIGRP   81

Configuring EIGRP   81
EIGRP Auto Summarization   82
Verifying EIGRP   82
Troubleshooting EIGRP   83
Configuration Example: EIGRP   83

Chapter 11   Single-Area OSPF   87

OSPF Routing: Mandatory Commands   87
Wildcard Masks   88
Using Wildcard Masks with OSPF Areas   88
OSPF Routing: Optional Commands   89
Loopback Interfaces   89
OSPF DR/BDR Election   89
Modifying OSPF Cost Metrics   89

OSPF Authentication: Simple   90
OSPF Authentication Using MD5 Encryption   90
OSPF Timers   91
Propagating a Default Route   91
Verifying OSPF Configuration   91
Troubleshooting OSPF   92
Configuration Example: Single-Area OSPF   93

Part V   Switches   97

Chapter 12   Configuring a Switch   99
Help Commands   99
Command Modes   99
Verifying Commands   100
Resetting Switch Configuration   100
Setting Host Names   101
Setting Passwords: 1900 Series Switches   101
Setting Passwords: 2900/2950 Series Switches   102
Setting IP Address and Default Gateway   102
Setting Interface Descriptions   103
Setting Duplex Settings: 1900 or 2900/2950 Series Switches   104
Setting Speed Settings: 2900/2950 Series Switches   104
Setting Web-Based Interface for Configuration: 1900 and 2900/
   2950 Series Switches   104
Managing the MAC Address Table: 1900 and 2900/2950 Series
   Switches   105
Configuring Static MAC Addresses   105
Port Security: 1900 Series Switches   105
Verifying Port Security   106
Configuration Example: 2900 Series Switch   107

Chapter 13   Spanning Tree Protocol and EtherChannel   111
Spanning Tree Protocol   111
   Spanning-Tree Verification   111
   Change Spanning-Tree Priority of a Switch   112
   Changing the Cost of Spanning Tree on an Interface   112
   Changing the State of Spanning Tree on an Interface   112
   Spanning Tree Portfast BPDU Guard Command   113
EtherChannel   113
   EtherChannel Configuration   113
   Verification of EtherChannel   114
   EtherChannel Tips   114

Chapter 14   VLANs   115

Displaying VLAN Information   115

Creating Static VLANs   116

Assigning Ports to VLANs   117

Assigning Ports Using the range Command (2950 Switch Only)   118

Saving VLAN Configurations   118

Erasing VLAN Configurations   119

Troubleshooting VLANs   120

Configuration Example: 2900 Switch Configuration   121

Chapter 15   VTP and Inter-VLAN Communication   125

Configuring ISL Trunks   125

Configuring Dot1Q Trunks   126

Verifying Trunking   126

VTP Configuration   127

Confirming VTP Configuration   128

Inter-VLAN Communication: Router-on-a-Stick   129

Router-on-a-Stick Tips   129

Configuration Example: VTP and Inter-VLAN Routing   130

Part VI   Network Administration and Troubleshooting   141

Chapter 16   Backing Up and Restoring Cisco IOS Software and Configurations   143

Boot System Commands   143

Cisco IOS Software Prerelease 12.0 Commands Versus Cisco IOS Software 12.x Commands   144

Backing Up Configurations   144

Restoring Configurations   145

Backing Up IOS to a TFTP Server   145

Restoring/Upgrading IOS from a TFTP Server   146

Restoring IOS from ROMmon Mode Using Xmodem   147

Restoring the IOS Using the ROMmon Environmental Variables and tftpdnld Command   150

Upgrading Catalyst 1900 Firmware with a TFTP Server   150

Copying IOS to TFTP Server   151

Firmware Upgrade of Catalyst 2950 Series Switches   152

Configuration Example: 2900 Series Switch   153

Chapter 17   Password Recovery Procedures and the Configuration Register   157

The Configuration Register   157

The Configuration Register: A Visual Representation   157

The Configuration Register—What the Bits Mean   158

The Boot Field   158
Console Terminal Baud Rate Settings   159
Changing the Console Line Speed—CLI   159
Changing the Console Line Speed—ROM Monitor
    Mode—1700/2600 Series   159
Password Recovery Procedures for Cisco Routers   160
Password Recovery for 1900 Series Switches   162
Password Recovery for 2900/2950 Series Switches   164

Chapter 18   CDP   167
Cisco Discovery Protocol   167

Chapter 19   Telnet   169
Telnet   169

Chapter 20   ping and traceroute   173
ICMP Redirect Messages   173
ping Command   173
ping   174
traceroute   175

Chapter 21   SNMP and Syslog   177
Configuring SNMP   177
Configuring Syslog   177

Chapter 22   Basic Troubleshooting   179
Viewing the Routing Table   179
Determining the Gateway of Last Resort   180
Determining the Last Routing Update   180
OSI Layer 3 Testing   180
OSI Layer 7 Testing   181
Interpreting the show interface Command   181
Clearing Interface Counters   181
Using CDP to Troubleshoot   182
traceroute Command   182
show controllers Command   182
debug Commands   182
Using Timestamps   183
OS IP Verification Commands   183
ip http server Command   184
netstat Command   184

Part VII   Managing IP Services   185

Chapter 23   NAT   187

Configuring Dynamic NAT: One Private to One Public Address
Translation   187
Configuring PAT: Many Private to One Public Address
Translation   189
Configuring Static NAT: One Private to One Permanent Public
Address Translation   191
Verifying NAT and PAT Configuration   192
Troubleshooting NAT and PAT Configuration   192
Configuration Example: Port Address Translation   192

Chapter 24   DHCP   197

Configuring DHCP   197
Verifying and Troubleshooting DHCP Configuration   198
Configuring a DHCP Helper Address   198
Configuration Example: DHCP   198

Part VIII   Wide-Area Networks   203

Chapter 25   HDLC and PPP   205

Configuring HDLC Encapsulation on a Serial Line   205
Configuring PPP on a Serial Line (Mandatory Commands)   205
Configuring PPP on a Serial Line (Optional Commands):
Compression   206
Configuring PPP on a Serial Line (Optional Commands):
Link Quality   206
Configuring PPP on a Serial Line (Optional Commands):
Multilink   206
Configuring PPP on a Serial Line (Optional Commands):
Authentication   206
Verifying or Troubleshooting a Serial Link/PPP
Encapsulation   208
Configuration Example: PPP   208

Chapter 26   ISDN and DDR   211

Configuring ISDN BRI: Setting the Switch Type   211
Configuring ISDN BRI: Setting SPIDs   212
Configuring ISDN PRI   212
Verifying ISDN Configuration   213
Troubleshooting ISDN   213
Configuring Legacy DDR   214
Configuring Dialer Profiles with DDR   215
Configuration Example: ISDN and DDR with No Dialer
Profiles   218

Chapter 27   Frame Relay   223

Configuring Frame Relay: Setting the Frame Relay
Encapsulation Type   223
Configuring Frame Relay: Setting the Frame Relay
Encapsulation LMI Type   224
Configuring Frame Relay: Setting the Frame Relay DLCI
Number   224
Configuring a Frame Relay Map   224
Configuring a Description of the Interface (Optional)   225
Configuring Frame Relay Using Subinterfaces   225
Verifying Frame Relay   226
Troubleshooting Frame Relay   226
Configuration Example: Frame Relay   227

Part IX   Network Security   233

Chapter 28   IP Access Control List Security   235

Access List Numbers   235
ACL Keywords   235
Creating Standard ACLs   236
Applying a Standard ACL to an Interface   237
Verifying ACLs   237
Removing an ACL   238
Creating Extended ACLs   238
The established Keyword   239
Creating Named ACLs   240
Using Sequence Numbers in Named ACLs   241
Removing Specific Lines in a Named ACL Using Sequence
Numbers   242
Sequence Number Tips   242
Including Comments About Entries in ACLs   242
Applying an Extended ACL to an Interface   243
Restricting Virtual Terminal Access   243
Configuration Example: Access Control Lists   244

Part X   Appendixes   247

Appendix A   Complete Configuration Example   249

Appendix B   Binary/Hex/Decimal Conversion Chart   265

Appendix C   Create Your Own Journal Here   275

Icons Used in This Book

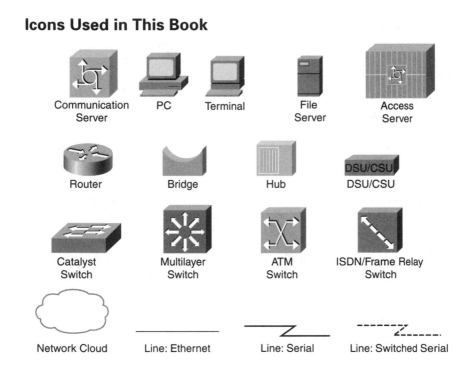

Command Syntax Conventions

The conventions used to present command syntax in this book are the same conventions used in the IOS Command Reference. The Command Reference describes these conventions as follows:

- **Boldface** indicates commands and keywords that are entered literally as shown. In actual configuration examples and output (not general command syntax), boldface indicates commands that are manually input by the user (such as a **show** command).
- *Italics* indicate arguments for which you supply actual values.
- Vertical bars I separate alternative, mutually exclusive elements.
- Square brackets [ ] indicate optional elements.
- Braces { } indicate a required choice.
- Braces within brackets [{ }] indicate a required choice within an optional element.

Introduction

Some of you might already be familiar with my first book for Cisco Press, the *CCNA Command Quick Reference*, a guide written to assist Cisco Networking Academy Program students in their studies toward CCNA certification. Now you might be asking yourself why I would open up an introduction for this book with a reference to another book. The answer is really quite simple. During the writing of that first book, Cisco Press received comments from some of their other partners. These other groups had heard of a command reference text being written for the Networking Academy, and they wanted to know when the "Industry" version would become available. That "Industry" version is what you are holding in your hands right now.

I have long been a fan of what I call the "Engineering Journal"—a small notebook that can be carried around and that contains little nuggets of information—commands that you forget, the IP addressing scheme of some remote part of the network, little reminders about how to do something you only have to do once or twice a year but is vital to the integrity and maintenance of your network. This journal has been a constant companion by my side for the past six years; I only teach some of these concepts every second or third year, so I constantly need to refresh commands and concepts, as well as learn new commands and ideas as they are released by Cisco. My journals were the best way for me to review, as they were written in my own words—words that I could understand. At least, I had better understand them, because if I didn't, I had only myself to blame.

The journals that I would create for my Networking Academy classes would always be different than the journals I would create when I was teaching from a different curriculum or if I was out in industry working on some production network. I could understand that the Networking Academy needed to split topics into smaller, more manageable chunks, but for me out in the real world, I needed these concepts to follow a different approach—I needed all of the routing protocols together in one place in my journals, and not spread across some two-year outline of knowledge.

Therefore, this book is my "Industry" edition of the engineering journal. It contains a different logical flow to the topics, one more suited to someone working in the field. Like topics are grouped together: routing protocols, switches, troubleshooting. More complex examples are given. New topics have been added, such as EtherChannel, Route Summarization, and Sequence Numbers in Named ACLs to name a few. I even added an appendix that is nothing but blank pages—a place for you to add in your own commands that you need in your world. We all recognize the fact that no network administrator's job can be so easily pigeonholed as to being just working with CCNA topics—you all have your own specific jobs and duties assigned to you. That is why you will find those blank pages at the end of the book—make this book your own; personalize it with what you need to make it more effective. That way your journal will not look like mine.

In my first book I specifically wrote about two Networking Academy instructors that were instrumental in pushing me to publish my Networking Academy journals. This time I have to mention another colleague, Hans Roth of Red River College in Winnipeg, Manitoba, Canada. At Networkers 2005, Hans knew I was about to start work on this book and that it would contain more information than the first book. As I began to write down what would and would not be in this book, that old feeling of nervousness began to creep into me. It was Hans who showed me something that would forever help me to relax and calm down; if ever I needed a break from the research or the writing or the editing, I just had to do what Hans showed me—how to juggle. Some of you may have seen me on the Friday of Networkers, at the end of the day, juggling in the Las Vegas Convention Center, waiting for Hans to finish his Techtorial. It was during that time that I was able to relax enough to know that I could finish this book, and now here it is for you to use and enjoy. Thank you Hans, for keeping me grounded. If you see me at any Networkers Conferences in the future, ask me and I may give you an impromptu speech on juggling as a means of relaxation—I now carry my juggling balls with me everywhere.

One final thank you I have to make is to another coworker—Colin Polanski of NAIT. Colin works with me in the Department of Telecommunications and is one of our wireless/satellite technology instructors. He is one of the smartest men I know. Recently he started taking my Cisco classes, in hopes of working towards his CCNA certification and getting a broader base of knowledge in the LAN wireless area. It was he who I constantly looked to when I needed someone to proof my journals. He was the perfect choice as a reviewer—someone with technical experience that was moving into this field and needed a bit of a reminder about commands and other CCNA topics. By his own words, his own journal has been written down three times: once after my lecture was done he wrote down commands, the second time after he tried the commands on the devices and he saw how they actually worked, and a third time to clean up the journal to make it something that he could easily use and follow. So to Colin I owe a big thanks and a copy of this book.

Networking Devices Used in the Preparation of This Book

In order to verify the commands that are in this book, I had to try them out on a few different devices. The following is a list of the equipment I used in the writing of this book:

- C1720 router running Cisco IOS Software Release 12.0(1)XA3, with a fixed Fast Ethernet interface, and a WIC-2A/S serial interface card
- C2501 router running Cisco IOS Software Release 11.0(10c)XB1, with a fixed Ethernet interface, and two fixed serial interfaces
- C2620 router running Cisco IOS Software Release 12.0(7)T, with a fixed Fast Ethernet interface, a WIC-2A/S serial interface card, and an NM-1E Ethernet interface
- WS-C1912-EN Catalyst switch, running Enterprise Edition software
- WS-C2912-XL Catalyst switch, running version 12.0(5.3)WC(1) Enterprise Edition software
- WS-C2950-12 Catalyst switch, running version C2950-C3.0(5.3)WC(1) Enterprise Edition software

These devices were not running the latest and greatest versions of IOS. Some of it is quite old.

Those of you familiar with Cisco devices will recognize that a majority of these commands work across the entire range of the Cisco product line. These commands are not limited to the platforms and IOS versions listed. In fact, these devices are in most cases adequate for someone to continue their studies into the CCNP level as well.

Who Should Read This Book?

This book is for those people preparing for the CCNA exam, whether through self study, on-the-job training and practice. There are also some handy hints and tips along the way to hopefully make life a bit easier for you in this endeavor. This book will also be useful to network professionals who are not preparing for the CCNA exam yet need a quick reference to reinforce or refresh networking concepts and commands. It is small enough that you will find it easy to carry around with you. Big heavy textbooks might look impressive on your bookshelf in your office, but can you really carry them all around with you when you are working in some server room or equipment closet somewhere?

Organization of This Book

This book follows what I feel is a logical approach to configuring a small- to medium-sized network. It is an approach that I give to my students when they invariably ask for some sort of outline to plan and then configure a network. Specifically, this approach is as follows:

- **Part I: TCP/IP**
    - **Chapter 1, "How to Subnet"** —An overview of how to subnet; examples of subnetting both a Class B and a Class C address; the use of the Binary AND operation; the Enhanced Bob Maneuver to subnetting.
    - **Chapter 2, "VLSM"**—An overview of VLSM; an example of using VLSM to make your IP plan more efficient.
    - **Chapter 3, "Route Summarization"** —Using Route Summarization to make your routing updates more efficient; an example of how to summarize a network; necessary requirements for summarizing your network.
- **Part II: Introduction to Cisco Devices**
    - **Chapter 4, "Cables and Connections"** —An overview of how to connect to Cisco devices, which cables to use for which interfaces, and the differences between the TIA/EIA 568A and 568B wiring standards for UTP.
    - **Chapter 5, "The Command-Line Interface"** —How to navigate through the Cisco IOS; IOS editing commands, keyboard shortcuts, and IOS help commands.
- **Part III: Configuring a Router**
    - **Chapter 6, "Configuring a Single Cisco Router"** —Commands needed to configure a single router: names, passwords, configuring interfaces, MOTD banners, IP host tables, saving and erasing your configurations.
- **Part IV: Routing**
    - **Chapter 7, "Static Routing"** —How to configure static routes in your internetwork.
    - **Chapter 8, "RIP"**—Commands on configuring and verifying RIP and RIPv2; how to see and clear your routing table.
    - **Chapter 9, "IGRP"**—Commands on configuring and verifying IGRP.
    - **Chapter 10, "EIGRP"**—Commands on configuring and verifying EIGRP.
    - **Chapter 11, "Single Area OSPF"** —Commands on configuring and verifying Single Area OSPF.

- **Part V: Switches**

  — **Chapter 12, "Configuring a Switch"** —Commands needed for configuration of Catalyst 1900/2900/2950 switches: names; passwords; IP addresses; default gateways; port speed and duplex; configuring static MAC addresses; managing the MAC address table; port security.

  — **Chapter 13, "Spanning Tree Protocol and EtherChannel"** —Verifying spanning tree; setting switch priorities; creating and verifying EtherChannel groups between switches.

  — **Chapter 14, "VLANs"**—Configuring static VLANs on 1900/2900/2950 switches; troubleshooting VLANs; saving and deleting VLAN information.

  — **Chapter 15, "VTP and Inter-VLAN Communication"**—Configuring a VLAN Trunk Link; VTP configuration; verifying VTP; inter-VLAN communication; router-on-a-stick and subinterfaces.

- **Part VI: Network Administration and Troubleshooting**

  — **Chapter 16, "Backing Up and Restoring Cisco IOS Software and Configurations"**—Boot commands for the IOS; backing up and restoring IOS using TFTP and Xmodem; firmware upgrades for Catalyst switches.

  — **Chapter 17, "Password Recovery and the Configuration Register"** —The configuration register; password recovery procedure for routers and switches.

  — **Chapter 18, "CDP"**—Commands related to customization and verification of CDP.

  — **Chapter 19, "Telnet"** —Commands used for Telnet to remotely connect to other devices.

  — **Chapter 20, "Ping and Traceroute"** —Commands for both **Ping** and extended **Ping**; the **Traceroute** command.

  — **Chapter 21, "SNMP and Syslog"** —Configuring SNMP; working with syslog.

  — **Chapter 22, "Basic Troubleshooting"** —Various **show** commands used to view the routing table; interpreting the **show** interface command; how to verify your IP settings using different operating systems.

- **Part VII: Managing IP Services**

  — **Chapter 23, "NAT"**—Commands relating to NAT and PAT configuration and verification.

  — **Chapter 24, "DHCP"**—Commands relating to DHCP configuration and verification.

- **Part VIII: Wide-Area Networks**

  — **Chapter 25, "HDLC and PPP"**—Configuring PPP; authentication of PPP using PAP or CHAP; compression in PPP; multilink in PPP; troubleshooting PPP; returning to HDLC encapsulation.

  — **Chapter 26, "ISDN and DDR"** —Configuring a BRI interface; configuring a PRI interface; verifying ISDN; configuring legacy DDR; verifying and troubleshooting legacy DDR.

- — **Chapter 27, "Frame Relay"** —Configuring basic Frame Relay; Frame Relay and subinterfaces; DLCIs; verifying and troubleshooting Frame Relay.
- **Part IX: Network Security**
  - — **Chapter 28, "IP Access Control List Security"** —Configuring standard ACLs; wildcard masking; creating extended ACLs; creating named ACLs; using sequence numbers in named ACLs; verifying and troubleshooting ACLs.
- **Part X: Appendixes**
  - — **Appendix A, "Complete Configuration Example"** —A diagram of a complex network using all technologies in this book is shown, with complete scripts of what commands are used to create this network—scripts are for every device in the network, and show both the command and the prompt.
  - — **Appendix B, "Binary/Hex/Decimal Conversion Chart"** —A chart showing numbers 0-255 in the three numbering systems of binary, hexadecimal, and decimal.
  - — **Appendix C, "Create Your Own Journal Here"** —Some blank pages for you to add in your own specific commands that may not be in this book.

Did I Miss Anything?

I am always interested to hear how my students, and now readers of my books, do on both vendor exams and future studies. If you would like to contact me and let me know how this book helped you in your certification goals, please do so. Did I miss anything? Let me know. I can't guarantee I'll answer your e-mail message, but I can guarantee that I will read all of them. My e-mail address is ccnaguide@empson.ca.

PART I

TCP/IP

Chapter 1   How to Subnet

Chapter 2   VLSM

Chapter 3   Route Summarization

How to Subnet

Class A–E Addresses

Class	Leading Bit Pattern	First Octet in Decimal	Notes
A	0xxxxxxx	0–127	0 is invalid 127 reserved for loopback testing
B	10xxxxxx	128–191	
C	110xxxxx	192–223	
D	1110xxxx	224–239	Reserved for multicasting
E	1111xxxx	240–255	Reserved for future use/testing

Formulae

2^N Where N is equal to number of bits borrowed	Number of total subnets created
$2^N - 2$	Number of valid subnets created
2^H Where H is equal to number of host bits	Number of total hosts per subnet
$2^H - 2$	Number of valid hosts per subnet

Class A Address	N	H	H	H
Class B Address	N	N	H	H
Class C Address	N	N	N	H

N = Network bits
H = Host bits
All 0s in host portion = Network or subnetwork address
All 1s in host portion = Broadcast address
Combination of 1s and 0s in host portion = Valid host address

Converting Between Decimal Numbers and Binary

In any given octet of an IP address, the 8 bits can be defined as follows:

2^7	2^6	2^5	2^4	2^3	2^2	2^1	2^0
128	64	32	16	8	4	2	1

To convert a decimal number into binary, you must turn on the bits (make them a 1) that would add up to that number, as follows:

$$187 = 10111011 = 128+32+16+8+2+1$$
$$224 = 11100000 = 128+64+32$$

To convert a binary number into decimal, you must add the bits that have been turned on (the 1s), as follows:

$$10101010 = 128+32+8+2 = 170$$
$$11110000 = 128+64+32+16 = 240$$

The IP address 138.101.114.250 is represented in binary as:

$$10001010.01100101.01110010.11111010$$

The subnet mask of 255.255.255.192 is represented in binary as:

$$11111111.11111111.11111111.11000000$$

Subnetting a Class C Network Using Binary

You have a Class C address of 192.168.100.0 /24. You need nine subnets. What is the IP plan of network numbers, broadcast numbers, and valid host numbers? What is the subnet mask needed for this plan?

You cannot use N bits, only H bits. Therefore, ignore 192.168.100. These numbers cannot change.

Step 1   Determine how many H bits you need to borrow to create nine valid subnets.

$$2^N - 2 \geq 9$$

N = 4, so you need to borrow 4 H bits and turn them into N bits.

Start with 8 H bits	HHHHHHHH
Borrow 4 bits	NNNNHHHH

Step 2   Determine the first valid subnet in binary.

0001HHHH	Cannot use subnet 0000 because it is invalid. Therefore, you must start with the bit pattern of 0001
0001**0000**	All 0s in host portion = subnetwork number
0001**0001**	First valid host number
.	
.	
.	
0001**1110**	Last valid host number
0001**1111**	All 1s in host portion = broadcast number

Step 3   Convert binary to decimal.

00010000 = 16	Subnetwork number
00010001 = 17	First valid host number
.	
.	
.	
00011110 = 30	Last valid host number
00011111 = 31	All 1s in host portion = broadcast number

Step 4   Determine the second valid subnet in binary.

0010HHHH	0010 = 2 in binary = second valid subnet
0010**0000**	All 0s in host portion = subnetwork number
0010**0001**	First valid host number
.	
.	
.	
0010**1110**	Last valid host number
0010**1111**	All 1s in host portion = broadcast number

Step 5   Convert binary to decimal.

00100000 = 32	Subnetwork number
00100001 = 33	First valid host number
.	
.	
.	
00101110 = 46	Last valid host number
00101111 = 47	All 1s in host portion = broadcast number

Step 6   Create IP plan table.

Valid Subnet	Network Number	Range of Valid Hosts	Broadcast Number
1	16	17–30	31
2	32	33–46	47
3	**48**	**49–62**	**63**

Notice a pattern? Counting by 16.

Step 7   Verify pattern in binary (third valid subnet in binary used here).

0011HHHH	Third valid subnet
00110000 = **48**	Subnetwork number
00110001 = **49**	First valid host number
.	
.	
.	
00111110 = **62**	Last valid host number
00111111 = **63**	Broadcast number

Step 8   Finish IP plan table.

Subnet	Network Address (0000)	Range of Valid Hosts (0001–1110)	Broadcast Address (1111)
0 (0000) invalid	192.168.100.0	192.168.100.1– 192.168.100.14	192.168.100.15
1 (0001)	192.168.100.16	192.168.100.17– 192.168.100.30	192.168.100.31
2 (0010)	192.168.100.32	192.168.100.33– 192.168.100.46	192.168.100.47
3 (0011)	192.168.100.48	192.168.100.49– 192.168.100.62	192.168.100.63
4 (0100)	192.168.100.64	192.168.100.65– 192.168.100.78	192.168.100.79
5 (0101)	192.168.100.80	192.168.100.81– 192.168.100.94	192.168.100.95
6 (0110)	192.168.100.96	192.168.100.97– 192.168.100.110	192.168.100.111
7 (0111)	192.168.100.112	192.168.100.113– 192.168.100.126	192.168.100.127
8 (1000)	192.168.100.128	192.168.100.129– 192.168.100.142	192.168.100.143
9 (1001)	192.168.100.144	192.168.100.145– 192.168.100.158	192.168.100.159
10 (1010)	192.168.100.160	192.168.100.161– 192.168.100.174	192.168.100.175
11 (1011)	192.168.100.176	192.168.100.177– 192.168.100.190	192.168.100.191
12 (1100)	192.168.100.192	192.168.100.193– 192.168.100.206	192.168.100.207
13 (1101)	192.168.100.208	192.168.100.209– 192.168.100.222	192.168.100.223

14 (1110)	192.168.100.**224**	192.168.100.**225**– 192.168.100.**238**	192.168.100.**239**
15 (1111) invalid	192.168.100.**240**	192.168.100.**241**– 192.168.100.**254**	192.168.100.**255**
Quick Check	**Always an even number**	**First valid host is always an odd #** **Last valid host is always even #**	**Always an odd number**

Use any nine subnets—the rest are for future growth.

Step 9   Calculate subnet mask.

The default subnet mask for a Class C network is as follows:

Decimal	Binary
255.255.255.0	11111111.11111111.11111111.00000000

1 = Network or subnetwork bit
0 = Host bit

You borrowed 4 bits; therefore, the new subnet mask is the following:

11111111.11111111.11111111.**1111**0000	255.255.255.**240**

NOTE: You subnet a Class B or a Class A network with exactly the same steps as for a Class C network; the only difference is that you start with more H bits.

Subnetting a Class B Network Using Binary

You have a Class B address of 172.16.0.0 /16. You need nine subnets. What is the IP plan of network numbers, broadcast numbers, and valid host numbers? What is the subnet mask needed for this plan?

You cannot use N bits, only H bits. Therefore, ignore 172.16. These numbers cannot change.

Step 1   Determine how many H bits you need to borrow to create nine valid subnets.

$2^N - 2 \geq 9$

N = 4, so you need to borrow 4 H bits and turn them into N bits.

Start with 16 H bits	HHHHHHHHHHHHHHHH (Remove the decimal point for now)
Borrow 4 bits	**NNNN**HHHHHHHHHHHH

Step 2   Determine the first valid subnet in binary (without using decimal points).

0001HHHHHHHHHHHH	
0001**000000000000**	Subnet number
0001**000000000001**	First valid host
.	
.	
.	
0001**111111111110**	Last valid host
0001**111111111111**	Broadcast number

Step 3   Convert binary to decimal (replacing the decimal point in the binary numbers).

0001**0000.00000000** = 16.0	Subnetwork number
0001**0000.00000001** = 16.1	First valid host number
.	
.	
.	
0001**1111.11111110** = 31.254	Last valid host number
0001**1111.11111111** = 31.255	Broadcast number

Step 4   Determine the second valid subnet in binary (without using decimal points).

0010HHHHHHHHHHHH	
0010**000000000000**	Subnet number
0010**000000000001**	First valid host
.	
.	

.	
0010**111111111**110	Last valid host
0010**111111111111**	Broadcast number

Step 5   Convert binary to decimal (returning the decimal point in the binary numbers).

0010**0000.00000000** = 32.0	Subnetwork number
0010**0000.00000001** = 32.1	First valid host number
.	
.	
.	
0010**1111.11111110** = 47.254	Last valid host number
0010**1111.11111111** = 47.255	Broadcast number

Step 6   Create IP plan table.

Valid Subnet	Network Number	Range of Valid Hosts	Broadcast Number
1	16.0	16.1–31.254	31.255
2	32.0	32.1–47.254	47.255
3	48.0	48.1–63.254	63.255

Notice a pattern? Counting by 16.

Step 7   Verify pattern in binary (third valid subnet in binary used here).

0011HHHHHHHHHHHH	Third valid subnet
0011**0000.00000000** = **48.0**	Subnetwork number
0011**0000.00000001** = **48.1**	First valid host number
.	
.	
.	
0011**1111.11111110** = **63.254**	Last valid host number
0011**1111.11111111** = **63.255**	Broadcast number

Step 8   Finish IP plan table.

Subnet	Network Address (0000)	Range of Valid Hosts (0001–1110)	Broadcast Address (1111)
0 (0000) invalid	172.16.**0.0**	172.16.**0.1**–172.16.**15.254**	172.16.**15.255**
1 (0001)	172.16.**16.0**	172.16.**16.1**–172.16.**31.254**	172.16.**31.255**
2 (0010)	172.16.**32.0**	172.16.**32.1**–172.16.**47.254**	172.16.**47.255**
3 (0011)	172.16.**48.0**	172.16.**48.1**–172.16.**63.254**	172.16.**63.255**
4 (0100)	172.16.**64.0**	172.16.**64.1**–172.16.**79.254**	172.16.**79.255**
5 (0101)	172.16.**80.0**	172.16.**80.1**–172.16.**95.254**	172.16.**95.255**
6 (0110)	172.16.**96.0**	172.16.**96.1**–172.16.**111.254**	172.16.**111.255**
7 (0111)	172.16.**112.0**	172.16.**112.1**–172.16.**127.254**	172.16.**127.255**
8 (1000)	172.16.**128.0**	172.16.**128.1**–172.16.**143.254**	172.16.**143.255**
9 (1001)	172.16.**144.0**	172.16.**144.1**–172.16.**159.254**	172.16.**159.255**
10 (1010)	172.16.**160.0**	172.16.**160.1**–172.16.**175.254**	172.16.**175.255**
11 (1011)	172.16.**176.0**	172.16.**176.1**–172.16.**191.254**	172.16.**191.255**
12 (1100)	172.16.**192.0**	172.16.**192.1**–172.16.**207.254**	172.16.**207.255**
13 (1101)	172.16.**208.0**	172.16.**208.1**–172.16.**223.254**	172.16.**223.255**
14 (1110)	172.16.**224.0**	172.16.**224.1**–172.16.**239.254**	172.16.**239.255**
15 (1111) invalid	172.16.**240.0**	172.16.**240.1**–172.16.**255.254**	172.16.**255.255**
Quick Check	**Always in form even #.0**	**First valid host is always even #.1** **Last valid host is always odd #.254**	**Always odd #.255**

Use any nine subnets—the rest are for future growth.

Step 9   Calculate the subnet mask.

The default subnet mask for a Class B network is as follows:

Decimal	Binary
255.255.0.0	11111111.11111111.00000000.00000000

1 = Network or subnetwork bit
0 = Host bit
You borrowed 4 bits; therefore, the new subnet mask is the following:

11111111.11111111.**1111**0000.00000000	255.255.**240**.0

Binary ANDing

Binary ANDing is the process of performing multiplication to two binary numbers. In the Decimal Numbering system, ANDing is addition: 2 and 3 equals 5. In Decimal, there are an infinite number of answers when ANDing two numbers together. However, in the Binary Numbering system, the AND function yields only two possible outcomes, based on four different combinations. These outcomes, or answers, can be displayed in what is known as a truth table:

0 and 0 = 0
1 and 0 = 0
0 and 1 = 0
1 and 1 = 1

You use ANDing most often when comparing an IP address to its subnet mask. The end result of ANDing these two numbers together is to yield the network number of that address.

Question 1
What is the network number of the IP address 192.168.100.115 if it has a subnet mask of 255.255.255.240?

Answer
Step 1   Convert both the IP address and the subnet mask to binary:

192.168.100.115 = 11000000.10101000.01100100.01110011

255.255.255.240 = 11111111.11111111.11111111.11110000

Step 2   Perform the AND operation to each pair of bits—1 bit from the address ANDed
to the corresponding bit in the subnet mask. Refer to the truth table for the
possible outcomes:

192.168.100.115 = 11000000.10101000.01100100.01110011

255.255.255.240 = <u>11111111.11111111.11111111.11110000</u>

ANDed result   = 11000000.10101000.01100100.01110000

Step 3   Convert the answer back into decimal:

11000000.10101000.01100100.01110000 = 192.168.100.112

The IP address 192.168.100.115 belongs to the 192.168.100.112 network when
a mask of 255.255.255.240 is used.

Question 2

What is the network number of the IP address 192.168.100.115 if it has a subnet mask of
255.255.255.192?

(Notice that the IP address is the same as in Question 1, but the subnet mask is different.
What answer do you think you will get? The same one? Let's find out!)

Answer

Step 1   Convert both the IP address and the subnet mask to binary:

192.168.100.115 = 11000000.10101000.01100100.01110011

255.255.255.192 = 11111111.11111111.11111111.11000000

Step 2   Perform the AND operation to each pair of bits—1 bit from the address ANDed
to the corresponding bit in the subnet mask. Refer to the truth table for the
possible outcomes:

192.168.100.115 = 11000000.10101000.01100100.01110011

255.255.255.192 = <u>11111111.11111111.11111111.11000000</u>

ANDed result   = 11000000.10101000.01100100.01000000

Step 3   Convert the answer back into decimal:

11000000.10101000.01100100.01110000 = 192.168.100.64

The IP address 192.168.100.115 belongs to the 192.168.100.64 network when a
mask of 255.255.255.192 is used.

So Why AND?

Good question. The best answer is to save you time when working with IP addressing and subnetting. If you are given an IP address and its subnet, you can quickly find out what subnetwork the address belongs to. From here, you can determine what OTHER addresses belong to the same subnet. Remember that if two addresses are in the same network or subnetwork, they are considered to be *local* to each other, and can therefore communicate directly with each other. Addresses that are not in the same network or subnetwork are considered to be *remote* to each other, and must therefore have a Layer 3 device (like a router or Layer 3 switch) between them in order to communicate.

Question 3

What is the broadcast address of the IP address 192.168.100.164 if it has a subnet mask of 255.255.255.248?

Answer

Step 1   Convert both the IP address and the subnet mask to binary:

192.168.100.164 = 11000000.10101000.01100100.10100100

255.255.255.248 = 11111111.11111111.11111111.11111000

Step 2   Perform the AND operation to each pair of bits—1 bit from the address ANDed to the corresponding bit in the subnet mask. Refer to the truth table for the possible outcomes:

192.168.100.164 = 11000000.10101000.01100100.10100100

255.255.255.248 = <u>11111111.11111111.11111111.11111000</u>

ANDed Result   = 11000000.10101000.01100100.10100000
              = 192.168.100.160 (Subnetwork #)

Step 3   Separate the network bits from the host bits:

255.255.255.248 = /29 = 1st 29 bits are network/subnetwork bits, therefore

*11000000.10101000.01100100.10100*000. The last three bits are host bits.

Step 4   Change all host bits to 1. Remember that all 1s in the host portion are the broadcast number for that subnetwork:

*11000000.10101000.01100100.10100*111

Step 5   Convert this number to decimal to reveal your answer:

11000000.10101000.01100100.10100111 = 192.168.100.167

The broadcast address of 192.168.100.164 is 192.168.100.167 when the subnet mask is 255.255.255.248.

Shortcuts in Binary ANDing

Remember when I said that this was supposed to save you time when working with IP addressing and subnetting? Well, there are shortcuts when you AND two numbers together:

- An octet of all 1s in the subnet mask will result in the answer being the exact same octet as in the IP address
- An octet of all 0s in the subnet mask will result in the answer being all 0s in that octet

Question 4

To what network does 172.16.100.45 belong, if its subnet mask is 255.255.255.0?

Answer

172.16.100.0

Proof

Step 1   Convert both the IP address and the subnet mask to binary:

172.16.100.45 = 10101100.00010000.01100100.00101101

255.255.255.0 = 11111111.11111111.11111111.00000000

Step 2   Perform the AND operation to each pair of bits – 1 bit from the address ANDed to the corresponding bit in the subnet mask. Refer to the truth table for the possible outcomes:

172.16.100.45 = 10101100.00010000.01100100.00101101

255.255.255.0 = <u>11111111.11111111.11111111.00000000</u>

10101100.00010000.01100100.00000000

= 172.16.100.0

Notice that the first three octets have the same pattern both before and after they were ANDed. Therefore, any octet ANDed to a subnet mask pattern of 255 is itself! Notice that the last octet is all 0s after ANDing. But according to the truth table, anything ANDed to a 0 is a 0. Therefore, any octet ANDed to a subnet mask pattern of 0 is 0! You should only have to convert those parts of an IP address and subnet mask to binary if the mask is not 255 or 0.

Question 5

To what network does 68.43.100.18 belong, if its subnet mask is 255.255.255.0?

Answer

68.43.100.0 (No need to convert here, mask is either 255s or 0s.)

Question 6

To what network does 131.186.227.43 belong, if its subnet mask is 255.255.240.0?

Answer

Based on the two shortcut rules, the answer should be

$$131.186.???.0$$

So now you only need to convert one octet to binary for the ANDing process:

$$227 = \qquad 11100011$$
$$240 = \qquad \underline{11110000}$$
$$11100000 = 224$$

Therefore the answer is 131.186.224.0.

The Enhanced Bob Maneuver for Subnetting (or How to Subnet Anything in Under a Minute)

Legend has it that once upon a time a networking instructor named Bob taught a class of students a method of subnetting any address using a special chart. This was known as the Bob Maneuver. These students, being the smart type that networking students usually are, added a row to the top of the chart and the Enhanced Bob Maneuver was born. The chart and instructions on how to use it follow. With practice, you should be able to subnet any address and come up with an IP plan in under a minute. After all, it's *just* math!

The Bob of the Enhanced Bob Maneuver was really a manager/instructor at SHL. He taught this maneuver to Bruce, who taught it to Chad Klymchuk. Chad and a coworker named Troy added the top line of the chart, enhancing it. Chad was first my instructor in Microsoft, then my coworker here at NAIT, and now is one of my Academy Instructors—I guess I am now his boss. And the circle is complete.

The Enhanced Bob Maneuver

	192	224	240	248	252	254	255	Subnet Mask
128	64	32	16	8	4	2	1	Target Number
8	7	6	5	4	3	2	1	Bit Place
	126	62	30	14	6	4	N/A	Number of Valid Subnets

Suppose that you have a Class C network and you need nine subnets.

1 On the bottom line (Number of Valid Subnets), move from *right* to *left* and find the closest number that is *bigger* than or *equal* to what you need:

Nine subnets—move to 14.

2. From that number (14), move up to the line called Bit Place.

Above 14 is bit place 4.

3. The dark line is called the *high-order line*. If you cross the line, you have to reverse direction.

You were moving right to left; now you have to move from left to right.

4. Go to the line called Target Number. Counting *from the left*, move over the number of spaces that the bit place number tells you.

Starting on 128, moving 4 places takes you to 16.

5. This target number is what you need to count by, starting at 0, and going until you hit 255 or greater. Stop before you get to 256:

0

16

32

48

64

80

96

112

128

144

160

176

192

208

224

240

~~256~~ Stop—too far!

6. These numbers are your network numbers. Expand to finish your plan.

Network #	Range of Valid Hosts	Broadcast Number
0 (invalid)	1–14	15
16	17–30 (17 is 1 more than network # 30 is 1 less than broadcast#)	31 (1 less than next network #)
32	33–46	47
48	49–62	63
64	65–78	79
80	81–94	95
96	97–110	111
112	113–126	127
128	129–142	143
144	145–158	159
160	161–174	175
176	177–190	191
192	193–206	207

Network #	Range of Valid Hosts	Broadcast Number
208	209–222	223
224	225–238	239
240 (invalid)	241–254	255

Notice that there are 14 subnets created from .16 to .224.

7. Go back to the Enhanced Bob Maneuver chart and look above your target number to the top line. The number above your target number is your subnet mask.

Above 16 is 240. Because you started with a Class C network, the new subnet mask is 255.255.255.240.

Variable-length subnet masking (VLSM) is the more realistic way of subnetting a network to make for the most efficient use of all of the bits.

Remember that when you perform classful (or what I sometimes call classical) subnetting, all subnets have the same number of hosts because they all use the same subnet mask. This leads to inefficiencies. For example, if you borrow 4 bits on a Class C network, you end up with 14 valid subnets of 14 valid hosts. A serial link to another router only needs 2 hosts, but with classical subnetting you end up wasting 12 of those hosts. Even with the ability to use NAT and private addresses, where you should never run out of addresses in a network design, you still want to ensure that the IP plan that you create is as efficient as possible. This is where VLSM comes in to play.

VLSM is the process of "subnetting a subnet" and using different subnet masks for different networks in your IP plan. What you have to remember is that you need to make sure that there is no overlap in any of the addresses.

IP Subnet Zero

When you work with classical subnetting, you always have to eliminate the subnets that contain either all zeros or all ones in the subnet portion. Hence, you always used the formula $2^N - 2$ to define the number of valid subnets created. However, Cisco devices can use those subnets, as long as the command **ip subnet-zero** is in the configuration. This command is on by default in Cisco IOS Software Release 12.0 and later; if it was turned off for some reason, however, you can re-enable it by using the following command:

```
Router(config)#ip subnet-zero
```

Now you can use the formula 2^N rather than $2^N - 2$.

2^N	Number of total subnets created	
~~$2^N - 2$~~	~~Number of valid subnets created~~	No longer needed because you have the **ip subnet-zero** command enabled
2^H	Number of total hosts per subnet	
$2^H - 2$	Number of valid hosts per subnet	

VLSM Example

You follow the same steps in performing VLSM as you did when performing classical subnetting.

Consider Figure 2-1 as you work through an example.

Figure 2-1   Sample Network Needing a VLSM Address Plan

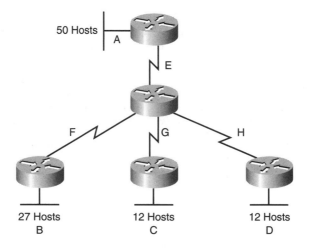

A Class C network—192.168.100.0/24—is assigned. You need to create an IP plan for this network using VLSM.

Once again, you cannot use the N bits—192.168.100. You can use only the H bits. Therefore, ignore the N bits, because they cannot change!

The steps to create an IP plan using VLSM for the network illustrated in Figure 2-1 are as follows:

Step 1   Determine how many H bits will be needed to satisfy the *largest* network.

Step 2   Pick a subnet for the largest network to use.

Step 3   Pick the next largest network to work with.

Step 4   Pick the third largest network to work with.

Step 5   Determine network numbers for serial links.

The remainder of the chapter details what is involved with each step of the process.

Step 1 Determine How Many H Bits Will Be Needed to Satisfy the *Largest* Network

A is the largest network with 50 hosts. Therefore, you need to know how many H bits will be needed:

If $2^H - 2$ = Number of valid hosts per subnet
Then $2^H - 2 \geq 50$
Therefore H = 6 (6 is the smallest valid value for H)

You need 6 H bits to satisfy the requirements of Network A.

If you need 6 H bits and you started with 8 N bits, you are left with 8 − 6 = 2 N bits to create subnets:

Started with: NNNNNNNN (these are the 8 bits in the fourth octet)
Now have: NNHHHHHH

All subnetting will now have to start at this reference point, to satisfy the requirements of Network A.

Step 2 Pick a Subnet for the Largest Network to Use

You have 2 N bits to work with, leaving you with 2^N or 2^2 or 4 subnets to work with:

NN = 00HHHHHH (The Hs = The 6 H bits you need for Network A)
01HHHHHH
10HHHHHH
11HHHHHH

If you add all zeros to the H bits, you are left with the network numbers for the four subnets:

00**000000** = .0
01**000000** = .64
10**000000** = .128
11**000000** = .192

All of these subnets will have the same subnet mask, just like in classful subnetting.

Two borrowed H bits means a subnet mask of:

11111111.11111111.11111111.11000000

or

255.255.255.192

or

/26

The /x notation represents how to show different subnet masks when using VLSM.

/8 means that the first 8 bits of the address are network, the remaining 24 bits are H bits.

/24 means that the first 24 bits are network, the last 8 are host—this is either a traditional default Class C address, or a traditional Class A network that has borrowed 16 bits, or even a traditional Class B network that has borrowed 8 bits!

Pick *one* of these subnets to use for Network A. The rest of the networks will have to use the other three subnets.

For purposes of this example, pick the .64 network.

00**000000** =	.0	
01**000000** =	.64	Network A
10**000000** =	.128	
11**000000** =	.192	

Step 3 Pick the Next Largest Network to Work With

Network B = 27 hosts

Determine the number of H bits needed for this network:

$$2^H - 2 \geq 27$$
$$H = 5$$

You need 5 H bits to satisfy the requirements of Network B.

You started with a pattern of 2 N bits and 6 H bits for Network A. You have to maintain that pattern.

Pick one of the remaining /26 networks to work with Network B.

For purposes of this example, select the .128/26 network:

10**000000**

But you need only 5 H bits, not 6. Therefore, you are left with:

10**N00000**

where:

10 represents the original pattern of subnetting.
N represents the extra bit.
00000 represents the 5 H bits you need for Network B.

Because you have this extra bit, you can create two smaller subnets from the original subnet:

10**000000**
10**100000**

Converted to decimal, these subnets are as follows:

10**000000** =.128
10**100000** =.160

You have now subnetted a subnet! This is the basis of VLSM.

Each of these sub-subnets will have a new subnet mask. The original subnet mask of /24 was changed into /26 for Network A. You then take one of these /26 networks and break it into two /27 networks:

10**000000** and 10**100000** both have 3 N bits and 5 H bits.

The mask now equals:

11111111.11111111.11111111.11100000

or

255.255.255.224

or

/27

Pick one of these new sub-subnets for Network B:

10**000000** /27 = Network B

Use the remaining sub-subnet for future growth, or you can break it down further if needed.

You want to make sure the addresses are not overlapping with each other. So go back to the original table.

00**000000** =	.0/26	
01**000000** =	.64/26	Network A
10**000000** =	.128/26	
11**000000** =	.192/26	

You can now break the .128/26 network into two smaller /27 networks and assign Network B.

00**000000** =	.0/26	
01**000000** =	.64/26	Network A
10**000000** =	.128/26	Cannot use because it has been subnetted
10**000000** =	.128/27	Network B
10**100000** =	.160/27	
11**000000** =	.192/26	

The remaining networks are still available to be assigned to networks, or subnetted further for better efficiency.

Step 4 Pick the Third Largest Network to Work With

Networks C and Network D = 12 hosts each

Determine the number of H bits needed for these networks:

$$2^H - 2 \geq 12$$
$$H = 4$$

You need 4 H bits to satisfy the requirements of Network C and Network D.

You started with a pattern of 2 N bits and 6 H bits for Network A. You have to maintain that pattern.

You now have a choice as to where to put these networks. You could go to a different /26 network, or you could go to a /27 network and try to fit them into there.

For the purposes of this example, select the other /27 network—.160/27:

> 10**100000** (The 1 in the third bit place is no longer bold, because it is part of the N bits.)

But you only need 4 H bits, not 5. Therefore you are left with:

> 101**N0000**

where:

> 10 represents the original pattern of subnetting.
> **N** represents the extra bit you have.
> **00000** represents the 5 H bits you need for Network B.

Because you have this extra bit, you can create two smaller subnets from the original subnet:

> 101**00000**
> 101**10000**

Converted to decimal, these subnets are as follows:

> 101**00000** = .160
> 101**10000** = .176

These new sub-subnets will now have new subnet masks. Each sub-subnet now has 4 N bits and 4 H bits, so their new masks will be:

> 11111111.11111111.11111111.11110000

or

> 255.255.255.240

or

> /28

Pick one of these new sub-subnets for Network C and one for Network D.

00**000000** =	.0/26	
01**000000** =	.64/26	Network A
10**000000** =	.128/26	Cannot use because it has been subnetted

10**000000** =	.128/27	Network B
10**100000** =	.160/27	Cannot use because it has been subnetted
101**00000**	.160/28	Network C
101**10000**	.176/28	Network D
11**000000** =	.192/26	

You have now used two of the original four subnets to satisfy the requirements of four networks. Now all you need to do is determine the network numbers for the serial links between the routers.

Step 5 Determine Network Numbers for Serial Links

Serial links between routers all have the same property in that they only need two addresses in a network—one for each router interface.

Determine the number of H bits needed for these networks:

$$2^H - 2 \geq 2$$
$$H = 2$$

You need 2 H bits to satisfy the requirements of Networks E, F, G, and H.

You have two of the original subnets left to work with.

For purposes of this example, select the .0/26 network:

00**000000**

But you need only 2 H bits, not 6. Therefore, you are left with:

00**NNNN00**

where:

00 represents the original pattern of subnetting.
NNNN represents the extra bits you have.
00 represents the 2 H bits you need for the serial links.

Because you have 4 N bits, you can create 16 sub-subnets from the original subnet:

00**000000** = .0/30
00**000100** = .4/30
00**001000** = .8/30
00**001100** = .12/30
00**010000** = .16/30
.
.
.
00**111000** = .56/30

$$00\mathbf{111100} = .60/30$$

You need only four of them. You can hold the rest for future expansion, or recombine them for a new, larger subnet:

$$00\mathbf{010000} = .16/30$$

.
.
.

$$00\mathbf{111000} = .56/30$$
$$00\mathbf{111100} = .60/30$$

These can all be recombined into the following:

$$00\mathbf{010000} = .16/28$$

Going back to the original table, you now have the following:

$00\mathbf{000000} =$	.0/26	Cannot use because it has been subnetted
$00\mathbf{000000} =$	.0/30	Network E
$00\mathbf{000100} =$	.4/30	Network F
$00\mathbf{001000} =$	.8/30	Network G
$00\mathbf{001100} =$	.12/30	Network H
$00\mathbf{010000} =$	.16/28	Future growth
$01\mathbf{000000} =$	.64/26	Network A
$10\mathbf{000000} =$	.128/26	Cannot use because it has been subnetted
$10\mathbf{000000} =$	.128/27	Network B
$10\mathbf{100000} =$	160/27	Cannot use because it has been subnetted
$10\mathbf{100000}$	160/28	Network C
$10\mathbf{110000}$	176/28	Network D
$11\mathbf{000000} =$	.192/26	Future growth

Looking at the plan, you can see that no number is used twice. You have now created an IP plan for the network, and have made the plan as efficient as possible, wasting no addresses in the serial links and leaving room for future growth. This is the power of VLSM!

CHAPTER 3

Route Summarization

Route summarization, or *supernetting*, is needed to reduce the amount of routes that a router advertises to its neighbor. Remember that for every route you advertise, the size of your update grows. It has been said that if there were no route summarization, the Internet backbone would have collapsed from the sheer size of its own routing tables back in 1997!

Routing updates, whether done with a distance vector or link-state protocol, grow with the number of routes you need to advertise. In simple terms, a router that needs to advertise 10 routes needs 10 specific lines in its update packet. The more routes you have to advertise, the bigger the packet. The bigger the packet, the more bandwidth the update takes, reducing the bandwidth available to transfer data. But with route summarization, you can advertise many routes with only one line in an update packet. This reduces the size of the update, allowing you more bandwidth for data transfer.

Also, when a new data flow enters a router, the router must do a lookup in its routing table to determine which interface the traffic must be sent out. The larger the routing tables, the longer this takes, leading to more used router CPU cycles to perform the lookup. Therefore, a second reason for route summarization is that you want to minimize the amount of time and router CPU cycles that are used to route traffic.

> **NOTE:** This example is a very simplified explanation of how routers send updates to each other. For a more in-depth description, I highly recommend you go out and read Jeff Doyle's book *Routing TCP/IP*, Volume I, Cisco Press. This book has been around for many years and is considered by most to be the authority on how the different routing protocols work. If you are considering continuing on in your certification path to try and achieve the CCIE, buy Doyle's book and memorize it. The second edition of Doyle's book was released im Autumn 2005.

Example for Understanding Route Summarization

Refer to Figure 3-1 to assist you as you go through the following explanation of an example of route summarization.

Figure 3-1   *Four-City Network Without Route Summarization*

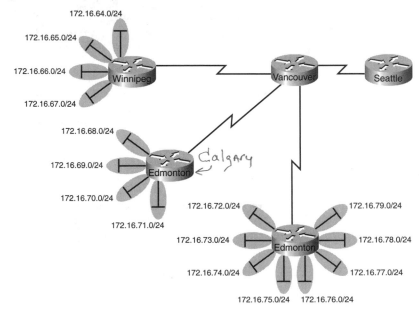

As you can see from Figure 3-1, Winnipeg, Calgary, and Edmonton each have to advertise internal networks to the main router located in Vancouver. Without route summarization, Vancouver would have to advertise 16 networks to Seattle. You want to use route summarization to reduce the burden on this upstream router.

Step 1: Summarize Winnipeg's Routes

To do this, you need to look at the routes in binary to see if there any specific bit patterns that you can use to your advantage. What you are looking for are common bits on the network side of the addresses. Because all of these networks are /24 networks, you want to see which of the first 24 bits are common to all four networks.

172.16.64.0 = *10101100.00010000.01000000*.00000000
172.16.65.0 = *10101100.00010000.01000001*.00000000
172.16.66.0 = *10101100.00010000.01000010*.00000000
172.16.67.0 = *10101100.00010000.01000011*.00000000
Common bits: *10101100.00010000.010000*xx

You see that the first 22 bits of the four networks are common. Therefore, you can summarize the four routes by using a subnet mask that reflects that the first 22 bits are common. This is a /22 mask, or 255.255.252.0. You are left with the summarized address of

172.16.64.0/22

This address, when sent to the upstream Vancouver router, will tell Vancouver: "If you have any packets that are addressed to networks that have the first 22 bits in the pattern of 10101100.00010000.010000xx.xxxxxxxx, then send them to me here in Winnipeg.

By sending one route to Vancouver with this supernetted subnet mask, you have advertised four routes in one line, instead of using four lines. Much more efficient!

Step 2: Summarize Calgary's Routes

For Calgary, you do the same thing that you did for Winnipeg—look for common bit patterns in the routes:

172.16.68.0 =	*10101100.00010000.010001*00.00000000
172.16.69.0 =	*10101100.00010000.010001*01.00000000
172.16.70.0 =	*10101100.00010000.010001*10.00000000
172.16.71.0 =	*10101100.00010000.010001*11.00000000
Common bits:	*10101100.00010000.010001*xx

Once again the first 22 bits are common. The summarized route is therefore:

172.16.68.0/22

Step 3: Summarize Edmonton's Routes

For Edmonton, you do the same thing that we did for Winnipeg and Calgary—look for common bit patterns in the routes:

172.16.72.0 =	*10101100.00010000.01001*000.00000000
172.16.73.0 =	*10101100.00010000.01001*001.00000000
172.16.74.0 =	*10101100.00010000 01001*010.00000000
172.16.75.0 =	*10101100.00010000 01001*011.00000000
172.16.76.0 =	*10101100.00010000.01001*100.00000000
172.16.77.0 =	*10101100.00010000.01001*101.00000000
172.16.78.0 =	*10101100.00010000.01001*110.00000000
172.16.79.0 =	*10101100.00010000.01001*111.00000000
Common bits:	*10101100.00010000.01001*xxx

For Edmonton, the first 21 bits are common. The summarized route is therefore:

172.16.72.0/21

Figure 3-2 shows what the network looks like, with Winnipeg, Calgary, and Edmonton sending their summarized routes to Vancouver.

Figure 3-2   Four-City Network with Edge Cities Summarizing Routes

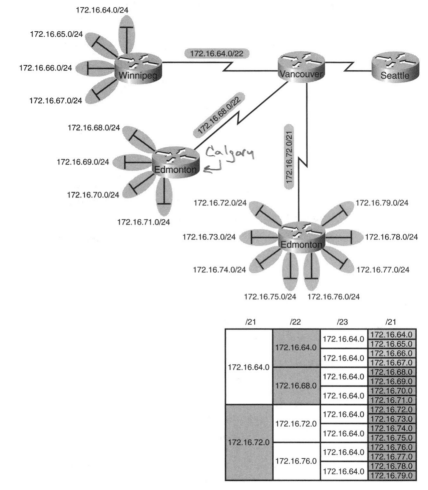

Step 4: Summarize Vancouver's Routes

Yes, you can summarize Vancouver's routes to Seattle. You continue in the same format as before. Take the routes that Winnipeg, Calgary and Edmonton sent to Vancouver and look for common bit patterns:

$$172.16.64.0 = \textit{10101100.00010000.01000000.00000000}$$
$$172.16.68.0 = \textit{10101100.00010000.01000100.00000000}$$
$$172.16.72.0 = \textit{10101100.00010000.01001000.00000000}$$
$$\text{Common bits: } \textit{10101100.00010000.0100xxxx}$$

Because there are 20 bits that are common, you can create one summary route for Vancouver to send to Seattle:

172.16.64.0/20

Vancouver has now told Seattle that in one line of a routing update, 16 different networks are being advertised. This is much more efficient than sending 16 lines in a routing update to be processed.

Figure 3-3 shows what the routing updates would look like with route summarization taking place.

Figure 3-3   Four-City Network with Complete Route Summarization

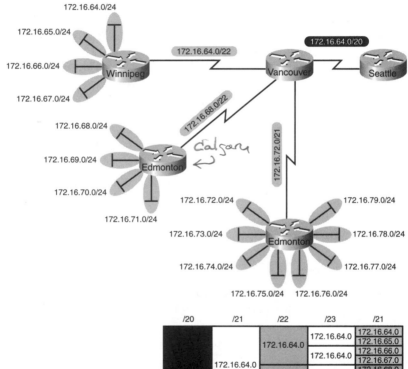

Route Summarization and Route Flapping

Another positive aspect of route summarization has to do with route flapping. *Route flapping* is when a network, for whatever reason (such as interface hardware failure or misconfiguration), goes up and down on a router, causing that router to constantly advertise changes about that network. Route summarization can help insulate upstream neighbors from these problems.

Consider router Edmonton from Figure 3-1. Suppose that network 172.16.74.0/24 goes down. Without route summarization, Edmonton would advertise Vancouver to remove that network. Vancouver would forward that same message upstream to Calgary, Winnipeg, Seattle, and so on. Now assume the network comes back online a few seconds later. Edmonton would have to send another update informing Vancouver of the change. Each time a change needs to be advertised the router must use CPU resources. If that route were to flap, the routers would constantly have to update their own tables, as well as advertise changes to their neighbors. In a CPU-intensive protocol such as OSPF, the constant hit on the CPU might make a noticeable change to the speed at which network traffic reaches its destination.

Route summarization enables you to avoid this problem. Even though Edmonton would still have to deal with the route constantly going up and down, no one else would notice. Edmonton advertises a single summarized route, 172.16.72.0/21, to Vancouver. Even though one of the networks is going up and down, this does not invalidate the route to the other networks that were summarized. Edmonton will deal with its own route flap, but Vancouver will be unaware of the problem downstream in Edmonton. Summarization can effectively protect or insulate other routers from route flaps.

Requirements for Route Summarization

To create route summarization, there are some necessary requirements:

- Routers need to be running a classless routing protocol, as they carry subnet mask information with them in routing updates. (Examples are RIP v2, OSPF, EIGRP, IS-IS, and BGP.)
- Addresses need to be assigned in a hierarchical fashion for the summarized address to have the same high-order bits. It does us no good if Winnipeg has network 172.16.64.0 and 172.16.67.0 while 172.16.65.0 resides in Calgary and 172.16.66.0 is assigned in Edmonton. No summarization could take place from the edge routers to Vancouver.

TIP: Because most networks use NAT and the 10 network internally, it is important when creating your network design that you assign network subnets in a way that they can be easily summarized. A little more planning now can save you a lot of grief later.

PART II

Introduction to Cisco Devices

Chapter 4   Cables and Connections

Chapter 5   The Command-Line Interface

Cables and Connections

This chapter provides information and commands concerning the following topics:

- Connecting a rollover cable to your router or switch
- Determining what your terminal settings should be
- Understanding the setup of different LAN connections
- Identifying different serial cable types
- Determining which cable to use to connect your router or switch to another device
- Verifying IP settings depending on your operating system
- 568A versus 568B cables

Connecting a Rollover Cable to Your Router or Switch

Figure 4-1 shows how to connect a rollover cable from your PC to a router or switch.

Figure 4-1   Rollover Cable Connections

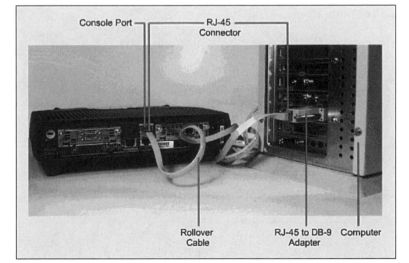

Terminal Settings

Figure 4-2 illustrates the settings that you should configure to have your PC connect to the router or switch.

Figure 4-2   PC Settings to Connect to a Router or Switch

LAN Connections

Table 4-1 shows the various port types and connections between LAN devices.

Table 4-1   LAN Connections

Port or Connection	Port Type	Connected To	Cable
Ethernet	RJ-45	Ethernet hub or Ethernet switch	RJ-45
T1/E1 WAN	RJ-48C/CA81A	T1 or E1 network	Rollover
Console	8 pin	Computer COM port	Rollover
AUX	8 pin	Modem	RJ-45
BRI S/T	RJ-48C/CA81A	NT1 device or private integrated network exchange (PINX)	RJ-45
BRI U WAN	RJ-49C/CA11A	ISDN network	RJ-45

Serial Cable Types

Figure 4-3 shows the DB-60 end of a serial cable that connects to a 2500 series router.

Figure 4-4 shows the newer smart serial end of a serial cable that connects to a smart serial port on your router.

Figure 4-5 shows examples of the male data terminal equipment (DTE) and the female data communications equipment (DCE) ends that are on the other side of a serial or smart serial cable.

Laptops released in the past few years come equipped with USB ports, not serial ports. For these newer laptops, you need a USB-to-serial connector, as illustrated in Figure 4-6.

Figure 4-3   Serial Cable (2500)

Figure 4-4   Smart Serial Cable (1700 or 2600)

Figure 4-5   V.35 DTE and DCE Cables

NOTE: CCNA focuses on *V.35 cables* for back-to-back connections between routers.

Figure 4-6   USB-to-Serial Connector for Laptops

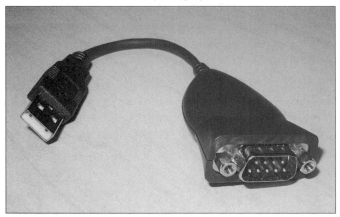

Which Cable to Use?

Table 4-2 describes which cable should be used when wiring your devices together. It is important to ensure you have proper cabling; otherwise, you might be giving yourself problems before you even get started.

Table 4-2   Determining Which Cables to Use When Wiring Devices Together

If device A has a:	And device B has a:	Then use this cable:
Computer COM port	Console of router/switch	Rollover
Computer NIC	Switch/hub	Straight-through
Computer NIC	Computer NIC	Crossover
Switch or hub port	Router's Ethernet port	Straight-through
Switch or hub port	Switch or hub port	Crossover (check for uplink button or toggle switch to defeat this)
Router's Ethernet port	Router's Ethernet port	Crossover
Computer NIC	Router's Ethernet port	Crossover
Router's serial port	Router's serial port	Cisco serial DCE/DTE cables

Table 4-3 lists the pinouts for straight-through, crossover, and rollover cables.

Table 4-3   Pinouts for Different Cables

Straight-Through Cable	Crossover Cable	Rollover Cable
Pin 1 – Pin 1	Pin 1 – Pin 3	Pin 1 – Pin 8
Pin 2 – Pin 2	Pin 2 – Pin 6	Pin 2 – Pin 7
Pin 3 – Pin 3	Pin 3 – Pin 1	Pin 3 – Pin 6
Pin 4 – Pin 4	Pin 4 – Pin 4	Pin 4 – Pin 5
Pin 5 – Pin 5	Pin 5 – Pin 5	Pin 5 – Pin 4
Pin 6 – Pin 6	Pin 6 – Pin 2	Pin 6 – Pin 3
Pin 7 – Pin 7	Pin 7 – Pin 7	Pin 7 – Pin 2
Pin 8 – Pin 8	Pin 8 – Pin 8	Pin 8 – Pin 1

568A Versus 568B Cables

There are two different standards released by the EIA/TIA group about UTP Wiring—568A and 568B. Although 568B is newer, and is the recommended standard, either one can be used. The difference between these two standards is pin assignments, not in the use of the different colors. The 568A standard is more compatible with voice connections and the Universal Service Order Codes (USOC) standard for telephone infrastructure in the USA. In both 568A and USOC standards, the blue and orange pairs are now on the center four pins; therefore, the colors match more closely with 568A than with the 568B standard.

So which one is preferred? Information here from the standards bodies on this matter is sketchy at best. 568B was traditionally widespread in the USA, whereas places like Canada and Australia use a lot of 568A. However, 568A is now becoming more dominant in the USA as well.

TIP: Use 568A in new installations, and 568B if connecting to an existing 568B system.

568A Standard				568B Standard			
Pin	Color	Pair	Description	Pin	Color	Pair	Description
1	white/green	3	RecvData +	1	white/orange	2	TxData +
2	green	3	RecvData -	2	orange	2	TxData -
3	white/orange	2	Txdata +	3	white/green	3	RecvData +
4	blue	1	Unused	4	blue	1	Unused
5	white/blue	1	Unused	5	white/blue	1	Unused
6	orange	2	TxData -	6	green	3	RecvData -
7	white/brown	4	Unused	7	white/brown	4	Unused
8	brown	4	Unused	8	brown	4	Unused

TIP: Odd pin numbers are always the striped wires.

A straight-through cable is one with both ends using the same standard (A or B).

A crossover cable is one that has 568A on one end, and 568B on the other end.

The Command-Line Interface

This chapter provides information and commands concerning the following topics:

- Navigating through command syntax and command modes
- The setup mode
- Keyboard help
- History commands
- **show** commands relating to these topics

Shortcuts for Entering Commands

To enhance efficiency, Cisco IOS Software has some shortcuts for entering commands. Although these are great to use in the real world, when it comes time to write a vendor exam, make sure you know the full commands, and not just the shortcuts.

`Router>enable` = `Router>enab` = `Router>en`	Entering a shortened form of a command is sufficient as long as there is no confusion over which command you are asking for

`Router#configure terminal`
is the same as:
`Router#config t`	

Using the ⎇Tab⎇ Key to Complete Commands

`Router#sh` ⎇Tab⎇ = `Router#show`	

Using the Question Mark for Help

The following output shows you how using the question mark can help you to work your way through a command and all of its parameters.

Router#?	Lists all commands available in the current command mode
Router#**c?** clear clock	Lists all the possible choices that start with **c**
Router#**cl?** clear clock	Lists all the possible choices that start with **cl**
Router#**clock**	
% Incomplete Command	Tells you that there are more parameters that need to be entered
Router#**clock ?** set	Shows all subcommands for this command. Sets the time and date
Router#**clock set 19:50:00 14 July 2003 ?** ⏎Enter	Pressing the ⏎Enter key confirms the time and date configured
Router#	No Error message/Incomplete Command message means the command was entered successfully

enable Command

Router>**enable** Router#	Moves user from user mode to privileged mode

exit Command

Router#**exit** or Router>**exit**	Logs a user off
Router(config-if)#**exit** Router(config)#	Moves you back one level
Router(config)#**exit** Router#	Moves you back one level

disable Command

Router#**disable** Router>	Moves you from privileged mode back to user mode

logout Command

Router#**logout**	Performs the same function as **exit**

Setup Mode

Starts automatically if no startup configuration present.

Router#**setup**	Enters startup mode from the command line

NOTE: The answer inside the square brackets [ ] is the default answer. If this is the answer you want, just press ⏎Enter.

Pressing Ctrl C at any time will end the setup process, shut down all interfaces, and take you to user mode (**Router>**).

NOTE: Setup mode *cannot* be used to configure an entire router. It does only the basics. For example, you can only turn on either RIPv1 or IGRP, but not OSPF or EIGRP. You cannot create ACLs here or enable NAT. You can assign an IP address to an interface, but not a subinterface. All in all, setup mode is very limiting.

Entering setup mode is not a recommended practice. Instead, you should use the command-line interface (CLI), which is more powerful:

Would you like to enter the initial configuration dialog? [yes] : **no**

Would you like to enable autoinstall? [yes]   **no**

Autoinstall is a feature that will try and broadcast out all interfaces to try and find a configuration. If you say **yes**, you will have to wait for a few minutes while it looks for a configuration to load. Very frustrating. Say **no**.

Keyboard Help

The keystrokes described in Table 5-1 are meant to help you in your editing of the config-uration. Because there are certain tasks that you want to do over and over again, Cisco IOS Software has in place certain keystroke combinations to help make the process more efficient.

Table 5-1   Keyboard Help

(A) (carat symbol; above the 6 key) See next row for an example	Shows you where you made a mistake in entering a command
```Router#confog t ^ % Invalid input detected at '^' marker. Router#config t Router(config)#```	
(Ctrl)(a)	Moves cursor to beginning of line
(Esc)(b)	Moves cursor back one word
(Ctrl)(b) (or ← left arrow)	Moves cursor back one character
(Ctrl)(e)	Moves cursor to end of line
(Ctrl)(f) (or → right arrow)	Moves cursor forward one character
(Esc)(f)	Moves cursor forward one word
(Ctrl)(z)	Moves you from any prompt back down to privileged mode
($)	Indicates that the line has been scrolled to the left
```Router#terminal no editing Router#```	Turns off the ability to use the previous keyboard shortcuts
```Router#terminal editing Router#```	Re-enables enhanced editing mode (can use above keyboard shortcuts)

History Commands

(Ctrl)(P) or (↑) (up arrow)	Recalls commands in the history buffer in a backward sequence, beginning with the most recent command
(Ctrl)(n) or (↓) (down arrow)	Returns to more recent commands in the history buffer after recalling commands with (Ctrl)(P) key sequence

`terminal history size` *number* See the next row for an example	Sets the number of commands in the buffer that can recalled by the router (maximum number is 256)
`Router#terminal history size 25`	Router will now remember the last 25 commands in the buffer
`Router#no terminal history size 25`	Sets history buffer back to 10 commands, which is the default

NOTE: The **history size** command provides the same function as the **terminal history size** command.

Be careful when you set the size to something larger than the default. By telling the router to keep the last 256 commands in a buffer, you are taking memory away from other parts of the router. What would you rather have: a router that remembers what you last typed in, or a router that routes as efficiently as possible?

show Commands

`Router#show version`	Displays information about current IOS
`Router#show flash`	Displays information about Flash memory
`Router#show history`	Lists all commands in the history buffer

NOTE: The last line of output from the **show version** command tells you what the configuration register is set to.

PART III

Configuring a Router

Chapter 6   **Configuring a Single Cisco Router**

Configuring a Single Cisco Router

This chapter provides information and commands concerning the following topics:

- Configuring a router, specifically:
  - Names
  - Passwords
  - Interfaces
  - MOTD banners
  - IP host tables
  - Saving and erasing your configurations
- **show** commands to verify the router configurations

Router Modes

`Router>`	User mode
`Router#`	Privileged mode
`Router(config)#`	Global configuration mode
`Router(config-if)#`	Interface mode
`Router(config-subif)#`	Subinterface mode
`Router(config-line)#`	Line mode
`Router(config-router)#`	Router configuration mode

TIP: There are other modes than these. Not all commands work in all modes. Be careful. If you type in a command that you know is correct—**show run**, for example—and you get an error, make sure that you are in the correct mode.

Global Configuration Mode

`Router>`	Limited viewing of config cannot make changes in this mode.
`Router#`	Can see config and move to make changes
`Router#config t` `Router(config)#`	Moves to global config mode. This prompt indicates that you can start making changes

Configuring a Router Name

This command works on both routers and switches.

`Router(config)#hostname Cisco` `Cisco(config)#`	Name can be any word you choose

Configuring Passwords

Works on both routers and switches.

`Router(config)#enable password cisco`	Sets enable password
`Router(config)#enable secret class`	Sets enable secret password
`Router(config)#line con 0`	Enters console-line mode
`Router(config-line)#password console`	Sets console-line mode password to **console**
`Router(config-line)#login`	Enables password checking at login
`Router(config)#line vty 0 4`	Enters vty line mode for all five vty lines
`Router(config-line)#password telnet`	Sets vty password to **telnet**
`Router(config-line)#login`	Enables password checking at login

Router(config)#**line aux 0**	Enters auxiliary line mode
Router(config-line)#**password backdoor**	Sets auxiliary line mode password to **backdoor**
Router(config-line)#**login**	Enables password checking at login

CAUTION: **enable secret password** is encrypted by default. **enable password** is not. For this reason, recommended practice is that you *never* use the **enable password**. Use only the **enable secret password** in a router configuration.

CAUTION: You cannot set both enable secret and enable password to the same password. Doing so defeats the use of encryption.

Password Encryption

Router(config)#**service password-encryption**	Applies a weak encryption to passwords
Router(config)#**enable password cisco**	Sets enable password to **cisco**
Router(config)#**line con 0**	...
Router(config-line)#**password Cisco**	Continue setting passwords as above
	...
Router(config)#**no service password-encryption**	Turns off password encryption

CAUTION: If you have turned on service password encryption, used it, and then turned it off, any passwords that you have encrypted will stay encrypted. New passwords will remain unencrypted.

show Commands

Router#**show ?**	Lists all **show** commands available
Router#**show interfaces**	Displays statistics for all interfaces
Router#**show interface serial 0**	Displays statistics for a specific interface, in this case Serial 0
Router#**show ip interface brief**	Displays a summary of all interfaces, including status and IP address assigned

`Router#show controllers serial 0`	Displays statistics for interface hardware. Statistics display if the clock rate is set and if the cable is DCE, DTE, or not attached
`Router#show clock`	Displays time set on device
`Router#show hosts`	Displays local host-to-IP address cache. These are the names and addresses of hosts on the network to which you can connect
`Router#show users`	Displays all users connected to device
`Router#show history`	Displays history of commands used at this edit level
`Router#show flash`	Displays info about Flash memory
`Router#show version`	Displays info about loaded software version
`Router#show arp`	Displays the ARP table
`Router#show protocols`	Displays status of configured Layer 3 protocols
`Router#show startup-config`	Displays configuration saved in NVRAM
`Router#show running-config`	Displays configuration currently running in RAM

Interface Names

One of the biggest problems that new administrators face is the interface names on the different models of routers. With all of the different Cisco devices that are in production networks today, some administrators are becoming confused on the names of their interfaces.

The following chart is a *sample* of some of the different interface names for various routers. This is by no means a complete list. Refer to the hardware guide of the specific router that you are working on to see the different combinations, or use the following command to see which interfaces are installed on your particular router:

`router#show ip interface brief`

Router Model	Port Location/ Slot Number	Slot/Port Type	Slot Numbering Range	Example
2501	On Board	Ethernet	Interface-type Number	ethernet0 (e0)
	On Board	Serial	Interface-type Number	serial0 (s0) & s1
2514	On Board	Ethernet	Interface-type Number	e0 & e1
	On Board	Serial	Interface-type Number	s0 & s1
1721	On Board	FastEthernet	Interface-type Number	fastethernet0 (fa0)
	Slot 0	WAC (WIN Interface Card) (Serial)	Interface-type Number	s0 & s1
1760	On Board	Fast Ethernet	Interface-type 0/port	fa0/0
	Slot 0	WIC/VIC (Voice Interface Card)	Interface-type 0/port	s0/0&s0/1 v0/0 & v0/1
	Slot 1	WIC/VIC	Interface-type 1/port	s1/0&s1/1 v1/0 & v1/1
	Slot 2	VIC	Interface-type 2/port	v2/0 & v2/1
	Slot 3	VIC	Interface-type 3/port	v3/0 & v3/1
2610	On Board	Ethernet	Interface-type 0/port	e0/0
	Slot 0	WIC (Serial)	Interface-type 0/port	s0/0 & s0/1
2611	On Board	Ethernet	Interface-type 0/port	e0/0 & e0/1
	Slot 0	WIC (Serial)	Interface-type 0/port	s0/0 & s0/1
2620	On Board	FastEthernet	Interface-type 0/port	fa0/0
	Slot 0	WIC (Serial)	Interface-type 0/port	s0/0 & s0/1
2621	On Board	FastEthernet	Interface-type 0/port	fa0/0 & fa 0/1
	Slot 0	WIC (Serial)	Interface-type 0/port	s0/0 & s0/1
1841	On Board	FastEthernet	Interface-type 0/port	fa 0/0 & fa 0/1
	Slot 0	High Speed WAN Interface Card (HWIC)/WIC/ VWIC	Interface-type 0/slot/port	s0/0/0 & s0/0/1
1841	Slot 1	HWIC/WIC/VWIC	Interface-type 0/slot/port	s0/1/0 & s0/1/1

Router Model	Port Location/ Slot Number	Slot/Port Type	Slot Numbering Range	Example
2801	On Board	FastEthernet	Interface-type 0/port	fa0/0 & fa 0/1
	Slot 0	VIC/VWIC (voice only)	Interface-type 0/slot/port	voice0/0/0 – voice0/0/3
	Slot 1	HWIC/WIC/VWIC	Interface-type 0/slot/port	0/1/0 – 0/1/3 (single-wide HWIC) 0/1/0 – 0/1/7 (double-wide HWIC)
	Slot 2	WIC/VIC/VWIC	Interface-type 0/slot/port	0/2/0 - 0/2/3
	Slot 3	HWIC/WIC/VWIC	Interface-type 0/slot/port	0/3/0 – 0/3/3 (single-wide HWIC) 0/3/0 - 0/3/7 (double-wide HWIC)
2811	Built into Chassis Front	USB	Interface-type port	usb0 & usb 1
	Built into Chassis Rear	FastEthernet Gigabit Ethernet	Interface-type 0/port	fa0/0&fa0/1 gi0/0 & gi0/1
	Slot 0	HWIC/HWIC-D/ WIC/VWIC/VIC	Interface-type 0/slot/port	s0/0/0&s0/0/1 fa0/0/0 & 0/0/1
	Slot 1	HWIC/HWIC-D/ WIC/VWIC/VIC	Interface-type 0/slot/port	s0/1/0&s0/1/1 fa0/1/0 & 0/1/1
	NME Slot	NM/NME	Interface-type 1/port	gi1/0&gi1/1 s1/0 & s1/1

Moving Between Interfaces

What happens in Column 1 is the same thing occurring in Column 2.

`Router(config)#int s0`	`Router(config)#int s0`	Moves to interface S0 mode
`Router(config-if)#exit`	`Router(config-if)#int e0`	In int S0, move to E0
`Router(config)#int e0`	`Router(config-if)#`	In E0 mode now
`Router(config-if)#`		Prompt does not change; be *careful*

Configuring a Serial Interface

`Router(config)#int s0/0`	Moves to interface Serial 0/0 mode
`Router(config-if)#description Link to ISP`	Optional descriptor of the link is locally significant
`Router(config-if)#ip address 192.168.10.1 255.255.255.0`	Assigns address and subnet mask to interface
`Router(config-if)#clock rate 56000`	Assigns a clock rate for the interface
`Router(config-if)#no shut`	Turns interface on

> **TIP:**   The **clock rate** command is used *only* on a *serial* interface that has a *DCE* cable plugged into it. There must be a clock rate set on every serial link between routers. It does not matter which router has the DCE cable plugged into it, or which interface the cable is plugged into. Serial 0 on one router can be plugged into Serial 1 on another router.

Configuring an Ethernet/Fast Ethernet Interface

`Router(config)#int fa0/0`	Moves to Fast Ethernet 0/0 interface mode
`Router(config-if)#description Accounting LAN`	Optional descriptor of the link is locally significant
`Router(config-if)#ip address 192.168.20.1 255.255.255.0`	Assigns address and subnet mask to interface
`Router(config-if)#no shut`	Turns interface on

Creating an MOTD Banner

`Router(config)#banner motd #  This is a secure`
`system. Authorized Personnel Only!  #`
`Router(config)#`
	# is known as a *delimiting character*. The delimiting character must surround the banner message and can be any character so long as it is not a character used within the body of the message

Setting the Clock Time Zone

`Router(config)#clock timezone EST -5`	Sets the time zone for display purposes. Based on coordinated universal time (Eastern Standard Time is 5 hours behind UTC)

Assigning a Local Host Name to an IP Address

`Router(config)#ip host london 172.16.1.3`	Assigns a host name to the IP address. After this assignment, you can use the host name instead of an IP address when trying to **Telnet** or **ping** to that address

`Router#ping london`
`=`
`Router#ping 172.16.1.3`	

TIP: The default port number in the **ip host** command is 23, or Telnet. If you want to Telnet to a device, just enter the IP host name itself:

`Router#london` = `Router#telnet london` = `Router#telnet 172.16.1.3`

no ip domain-lookup Command

Router(config)#no ip domain-lookup Router(config)#	Turns off trying to automatically resolve an unrecognized command to a local host name

> **TIP:** Ever type in a command incorrectly and are left having to wait for a minute or two as the router tries to *translate* your command to a domain server of 255.255.255.255? The router is set by default to try to resolve any word that is not a command to a DNS server at address 255.255.255.255. If you are not going to set up DNS, turn this feature off to save you time as you type, especially if you are a poor typist.

logging synchronous Command

Router(config)#line con 0	
Router(config-line)#logging synchronous	Turns on synchronous logging. Information items sent to console will not interrupt the command you are typing. The command will be moved to a new line

> **TIP:** Ever try to type in a command and an informational line appears in the middle of what you were typing? Lose your place? Do not know where you are in the command, so you just press ⏎Enter and start all over? The **logging synchronous** command will tell the router that if any informational items get displayed on the screen, your prompt and command line should be moved to a new line, so as not to confuse you.

The informational line does not get inserted into the middle of the command you are trying to type. If you were to continue typing, the command would execute properly, even though it looks wrong on the screen.

exec-timeout Command

`Router(config)#line con 0`	
`Router(config-line)#exec-timeout 0 0`	Sets time limit when console automatically logs off. Set to **0 0** (minutes seconds) means console never logs off
`Router(config-line)#`	

> **TIP:** **exec-timeout 0 0** is great for a lab because the console never logs out. This bad security is very dangerous in the real world.

Saving Configurations

`Router#copy run start`	Saves the running-config to local NVRAM
`Router#copy run tftp`	Saves the running-config remotely to TFTP server

Erasing Configurations

`Router#erase start`	Deletes the startup-config file from NVRAM

> **TIP:** Running-config is still in dynamic memory. Reload the router to clear the running-config.

Configuration Example: Basic Router Configuration

Figure 6-1 shows the network topology for the configuration that follows, which shows a basic router configuration using the commands covered in this chapter.

Figure 6-1   Network Topology for Basic Router Configuration

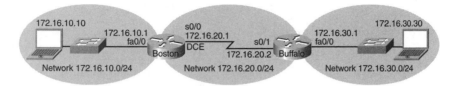

Boston Router

Router>**en**	Enters privileged mode
Router#**clock set 18:30:00 15 Nov 2004**	Sets local time on router
Router#**config t**	Enters global config mode
Router(config)#**hostname Boston**	Sets router name to **Boston**
Boston(config)#**no ip domain-lookup**	Turns off name resolution on unrecognized commands (spelling mistakes)
Boston(config)#**banner motd #** This is the Boston Router. Authorized Access Only #	Creates an MOTD banner
Boston(config)#**clock timezone EST –5**	Sets time zone to Eastern Standard Time (–5 from UTC)
Boston(config)#**enable secret cisco**	Enables secret password set to **cisco**
Boston(config)#**service password-encryption**	Passwords will be given weak encryption
Boston(config)#**line con 0**	Enters line console mode
Boston(config-line)#**logging sync**	Commands will not be interrupted by unsolicited messages
Boston(config-line)#**password class**	Sets password to **class**

`Boston(config-line)#login`	Enables password checking at login
`Boston(config-line)#line vty 0 4`	Moves to virtual Telnet lines 0 through 4
`Boston(config-line)#password class`	Sets password to **class**
`Boston(config-line)#login`	Enables password checking at login
`Boston(config-line)#line aux 0`	Moves to line auxiliary mode
`Boston(config-line)#password class`	Sets password to **class**
`Boston(config-line)#login`	Enables password checking at login
`Boston(config-line)#exit`	Moves back to global config mode
`Boston(config)#no service password-encryption`	Turns off password encryption
`Boston(config)#int fa 0/0`	Moves to Fast Ethernet 0/0 mode
`Boston(config-if)#desc Engineering LAN`	Sets locally significant description of the interface
`Boston(config-if)#ip address 172.16.10.1 255.255.255.0`	Assigns IP address and subnet mask to the interface
`Boston(config-if)#no shut`	Turns on the interface
`Boston(config-if)#int s0/0`	Moves directly to Serial 0/0 mode
`Boston(config-if)#desc Link to Buffalo Router`	Sets locally significant description of the interface
`Boston(config-if)#ip address 172.16.20.1 255.255.255.0`	Assigns IP address and subnet mask to the interface
`Boston(config-if)#clock rate 56000`	Sets a clock rate for serial transmission. DCE cable must be plugged into this interface
`Boston(config-if)#no shut`	Turns on the interface

`Boston(config-if)#exit`	Moves back to global config mode
`Boston(config)#ip host buffalo 172.16.20.2`	Sets a local host name resolution to IP address 172.16.20.2
`Boston(config)#exit`	Moves back to privileged mode
`Boston#copy run start`	Saves running-config to NVRAM

—

PART IV

Routing

Chapter 7   **Static Routing**

Chapter 8   **RIP**

Chapter 9   **IGRP**

Chapter 10   **EIGRP**

Chapter 11   **Single Area OSPF**

Static Routing

This chapter provides information and commands concerning the following topics:

- Configuring a static route on a router
- Configuring a default route on a router
- Verifying static routes

Static Routing

When using the **ip route** command, you can identify where packets should be routed to in two ways:

- The next-hop address
- The exit interface

Both ways are shown in both the "Configuration Example: Static Routes" section and the "Default Routing" section.

`Router(config)#ip route 172.16.20.0` `255.255.255.0 172.16.10.2`	172.16.20.0 = destination network 255.255.255.0 = subnet mask 172.16.10.2 = next-hop address Read this to say: To get to the destination network of 172.16.20.0, with a subnet mask of 255.255.255.0, send all packets to 172.16.10.2
`Router(config)#ip route 172.16.20.0` `255.255.255.0 s0/0`	172.16.20.0 = destination network 255.255.255.0 = subnet mask s0/0 = exit interface Read this to say: To get to the destination network of 172.16.20.0, with a subnet mask of 255.255.255.0, send all packets out interface Serial 0/0

The permanent Keyword (Optional)

`Router(config)#ip route 172.16.20.0` `255.255.255.0 172.16.10.2 permanent`	Specifies that the route will not be removed, even if the interface shuts down

Without the **permanent** keyword in a static route statement, a static route will be removed if an interface goes down. If you don't tighten those serial cables or if you have a bad connector on a UTP cable, a cable can easily become loose, causing an interface to go down. But plugging the cable back in does not add that static route back into the routing table. The only way to get that route back into the table is to reload the router or use the **permanent** keyword in your **ip route** command. This option is especially useful when the night janitor knocks a cable loose and replaces it, hoping no one will notice.... Can your network afford to lose a route for a few hours until the next morning when you or your IT staff comes in to work? The **permanent** keyword is also useful in helping to avoid constant shortest path first (SPF) calculations in OSPF when there is a flapping link; if the link goes down, the route will stay in the routing table.

However, you must be careful when using this optional keyword. You might want that route to be removed from the routing table. You might also want to know why the night janitor was in your wiring closet in the first place.

Static Routes and Administrative Distance (Optional)

`Router(config)#ip route 172.16.20.0` `255.255.255.0 172.16.10.2 200`	Specifies that an administrative distance of 200 has been assigned to this route.

NOTE: By default, a static route is assigned an administrative distance (AD) of 1. Administrative distance rates the "trustworthiness" of a route. AD is a number from 0-255, where 0 is absolutely trusted, and 255 cannot be trusted at all. Therefore, an AD of 1 is an extremely reliable rating, with only an AD of 0 being better. An AD of 0 is assigned to a directly connected route. The following table lists the administrative distance for each type of route.

Route Type	Administrative Distance
Connected	0
Static	1
EIGRP Summary Route	5
EBGP	20
EIGRP (Internal)	90
IGRP	100

Route Type	Administrative Distance
OSPF	110
IS-IS	115
RIP	120
EGP	140
On-Demand Routing	160
EIGRP (External)	170
iBGP (External)	200
Unknown	255

TIP: By default, a static route will always be used instead of a routing protocol. By adding an AD number to your **ip route** statement, however, you can effectively create a backup route to your routing protocol. If your network is using EIGRP, and you need a backup route, add a static route with an AD greater than 90. EIGRP will be used because its AD is better (lower) than the static route. But if EIGRP goes down, the static route will be used in its place. This is known as a *floating static route*. See Appendix A, "Complete Configuration Example," for an example where a floating static route is used as a backup route.

Default Routing

`Router(config)#ip route 0.0.0.0 0.0.0.0 172.16.10.2`	Send all packets destined for networks not in my routing table to 172.16.10.2
`Router(config)#ip route 0.0.0.0 0.0.0.0 s0/0`	Send all packets destined for networks not in my routing table out my Serial 0/0 interface

Verifying Static Routes

`Router#show ip route`	Displays contents of IP routing table

NOTE: The codes to the left of the routes in the table tell you from where the router learned the routes. A static route is described by the letter S.

Configuration Example: Static Routes

Figure 7-1 shows the network topology for the configuration that follows, which shows how to configure static routes using the commands covered in this chapter.

Figure 7-1   Network Topology for Static Route Configuration

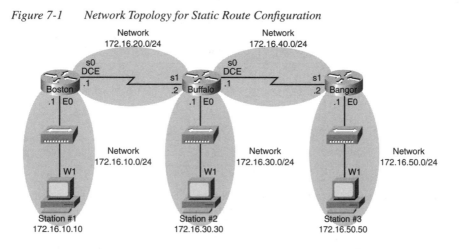

NOTE: The host name, password, and interfaces have all been configured as per the configuration in the Chapter 6 configuration example.

Boston Router

Boston>**en**	
Boston#**config t**	
Boston(config)#**ip route 172.16.30.0 255.255.255.0 172.16.20.2**	Configures a static route using the next-hop address
Boston(config)#**ip route 172.16.40.0 255.255.255.0 172.16.20.2**	
Boston(config)#**ip route 172.16.50.0 255.255.255.0 172.16.20.2**	
Boston(config)#**exit**	
Boston#**copy run start**	

Buffalo Router

Buffalo>**en**	
Buffalo#**config t**	
Buffalo(config)#**ip route 172.16.10.0 255.255.255.0 s1**	Configures a static route using the exit interface
Buffalo(config)#**ip route 172.16.50.0 255.255.255.0 s0**	
Boston(config)#**exit**	
Boston#**copy run start**	

Bangor Router

Bangor>**en**	
Bangor#**config t**	
Bangor(config)#**ip route 0.0.0.0 0.0.0.0 s1**	Configures a static route using the default route
Bangor(config)#**exit**	
Bangor#**copy run start**	

CHAPTER 8

RIP

This chapter provides information and commands concerning the following topics:

- Mandatory and optional commands for configuring the Routing Information Protocol (RIP)
- Mandatory and optional commands for configuring RIP Version 2 (RIP-2)

IP Classless

`Router(config)#ip classless`	Instructs IOS to forward packets destined for an unknown subnet to the best supernet route
`Router(config)#no ip classless`	Turns off the **ip classless** command

NOTE: A supernet route is a route that covers a range of subnets with a single entry.

NOTE: The **ip classless** command is enabled by default in Cisco IOS Software Release 11.3 and later.

RIP Routing: Mandatory Commands

`Router(config)#router rip`	Enables RIP as a routing protocol
`Router(config-router)#network w.x.y.z`	*w.x.y.z* is the network number of the *directly connected* network you want to advertise

NOTE: You need to advertise only the classful network number, not a subnet:

`Router(config-router)#network 172.16.0.0`

not

`Router(config-router)#network 172.16.10.0`

If you advertise a subnet, you will not receive an error message, because the router will automatically convert the subnet to the classful network address.

RIP Routing: Optional Commands

`Router(config)#no router rip`	Turns off the RIP routing process
`Router(config-router)#no network w.x.y.z`	Removes network *w.x.y.z* from the RIP routing process
`Router(config-router)#passive-interface s0/0`	RIP updates will not be sent out this interface
`Router(config-router)#neighbor a.b.c.d`	Defines a specific neighbor with which to exchange information
`Router(config-router)#no ip split-horizon`	Turns off split horizon (on by default)
`Router(config-router)#ip split-horizon`	Re-enables split horizon
`Router(config-router#timers basic 30 90 180 270 360`	Changes timers in RIP: 30 = Update timer (in seconds) 90 = Invalid timer (in seconds) 180 = Hold-down timer (in seconds) 270 = Flush timer (in seconds) 360 = Sleep time (in milliseconds)
`Router(config-router)#maximum-paths x`	Limits the number of paths for load balancing to *x* (4 = default, 6 = maximum)
`Router(config-router)#default-information originate`	Generates a default route into RIP

RIP Version 2

NOTE: RIP-2 is not currently part of the CCNA certification exam. Commands are listed here for reference only.

`Router(config-router)#version 2`	RIP will now send and receive RIP-2 packets globally
`Router(config-if)#ip rip send version 1`	Interface will send only RIP-1 packets
`Router(config-if)#ip rip send version 2`	Interface will send only RIP-2 packets
`Router(config-if)#ip rip send version 1 2`	Interface will send both RIP-1 and RIP-2 packets
`Router(config-if)#ip rip receive version 1`	Interface will receive only RIP-1 packets
`Router(config-if)#ip rip receive version 2`	Interface will receive only RIP-2 packets
`Router(config-if)#ip rip receive version 1 2`	Interface will receive both RIP-1 and RIP-2 packets

Troubleshooting RIP Issues

`Router#debug ip rip`	Displays all RIP activity in real time
`Router#show ip rip database`	Displays contents of the RIP database

RIP Version 2: Mandatory Commands

`Router(config)#router rip`	Turns on the RIP routing process; the same command as used for RIP Version 1 (RIP-1)
`Router(config-router)#version 2`	Turns on Version 2 of the routing process. Version 1 is default
`Router(config-router)#network w.x.y.z`	w.x.y.z is the network number of the *directly connected classful network* you want to advertise

RIP Version 2: Optional Commands

`Router(config-router)#no version 2`	Changes back to RIP-1
`Router(config-router)#version 1`	Changes RIP routing to RIP-1
`Router(config-router)#no auto-summary`	RIP-2 summarizes networks at the classful boundary. This command turns autosummarization off
`Router(config-router)#auto-summary`	Re-enables autosummarization at the classful boundary

Configuration Example: RIP-2 Routing

Figure 8-1 shows the network topology for the configuration that follows, which shows how to configure RIP-2 using the commands covered in this chapter.

Figure 8-1   Network Topology for RIP-2 Routing Configuration

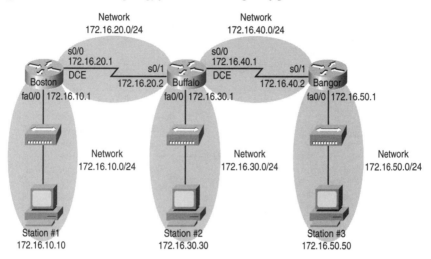

NOTE: The host name, password, and interfaces have all been configured as per the configuration example in Chapter 6, "Configuring a Single Cisco Router," of this book.

Boston Router

`Boston>`**`en`**	
`Boston#`**`config t`**	
`Boston(config)#`**`router rip`**	Enables RIP routing
`Boston(config-router)#`**`version 2`**	Enables RIP-2
`Boston(config-router)#`**`network 172.16.0.0`**	Advertises directly connected networks (classful address only)
`Boston(config-router)#`**`no auto-summary`**	Turns off autosummarization
`Boston(config-router)#`**`exit`**	
`Boston(config)#`**`exit`**	
`Boston#`**`copy run start`**	

Buffalo Router

`Buffalo>`**`en`**	
`Buffalo#`**`config t`**	
`Buffalo(config)#`**`router rip`**	Enables RIP routing
`Buffalo(config-router)#`**`version 2`**	Enables RIP-2
`Buffalo(config-router)#`**`network 172.16.0.0`**	Advertises directly connected networks (classful address only)
`Buffalo(config-router)#`**`no auto-summary`**	Turns off autosummarization
`Buffalo(config-router)#`Ctrl z	Exits back to privileged mode
`Buffalo#`**`copy run start`**	

Bangor Router

`Bangor>`**`en`**	
`Bangor#`**`config t`**	
`Bangor(config)#`**`router rip`**	Enables RIP routing
`Bangor(config-router)#`**`version 2`**	Enables RIP-2
`Bangor(config-router)#`**`network 172.16.0.0`**	Advertises directly connected networks (classful address only)
`Bangor(config-router)#`**`no auto-summary`**	Turns off autosummarization
`Bangor(config-router)#`Ctrl z	Exits back to privileged mode
`Bangor#`**`copy run start`**	

This chapter provides information and commands concerning the following topics:

- Mandatory and optional commands for configuring the Interior Gateway Routing Protocol (IGRP)

IGRP Routing: Mandatory Commands

`Router(config)#router igrp` *as-number*	Enables IGRP routing process. The autonomous system number (*AS-number*) used in the IGRP routing process *must match* all other routers that are going to share routing updates in order for communication to take place
`Router(config-router)#network` *w.x.y.z*	*w.x.y.z* is the network number of the *directly connected* network you want to advertise

NOTE: You need to advertise only the classful network number, not a subnet:

Router(config-router)#**network 172.16.0.0**

not

Router(config-router)#**network 172.16.10.0**

If you advertise a subnet, you will not receive an error message, because the router will automatically convert the subnet to the classful network address.

IGRP Routing: Optional Commands

`Router(config)#no router igrp as-number`	Disables the IGRP routing process
`Router(config-router)#no network w.x.y.z`	Removes network *w.x.y.z* from the IGRP routing process
`Router(config-if)#bandwidth x`	Sets the bandwidth of this interface to *x* kilobits to allow IGRP to make a better routing decision
`Router(config-router)#variance x`	Allows IGRP to accept unequal-cost routes

TIP: The **bandwidth** command is used for metric calculations only. It does not change interface performance.

Troubleshooting IGRP Issues

`Router#debug ip igrp events`	Shows all IGRP events in real time
`Router#debug ip igrp transactions`	Shows IGRP updates between routers

CAUTION: IGRP as a routing protocol is no longer supported by Cisco as of Cisco IOS Software Release 12.3. If you are using Cisco IOS 12.3 or newer code, you must use either Enhanced IGRP (EIGRP) or one of the other standards—RIP-1, RIP-2, or OSPF.

This chapter provides information and commands concerning the following topics:

- Configuring EIGRP
- EIGRP autosummarization
- Verifying EIGRP
- Troubleshooting EIGRP

Configuring EIGRP

`Router(config)#`**`router eigrp 100`**	Turns on the EIGRP process **100** is the autonomous system (AS) number, which can be a number between 1 and 65535 All routers in the same AS must use the same AS number
`Router(config-router)#`**`network 10.0.0.0`**	Specifies which network to advertise in EIGRP
`Router(config-router)#`**`eigrp log-neighbor-changes`**	Logs any changes to an EIGRP neighbor adjacency

TIP: The **eigrp log-neighbor-changes** command, although optional, is recommended to help with troubleshooting.

`Router(config-router)#`**`no network 10.0.0.0`**	Removes the network from the EIGRP process
`Router(config)#`**`no eigrp 100`**	Disables routing process 100
`Router(config-if)#`**`bandwidth x`**	Sets the bandwidth of this interface to x kilobits to allow EIGRP to make a better routing decision

TIP: The **bandwidth** command is used for metric calculations only. It does not change interface performance.

EIGRP Auto Summarization

Router(config-router)#**no auto-summary**	Turns off the auto-summarization feature. Networks are summarized at the classful boundary by default
Router(config)#**int fa 0/0**	
Router(config-if)#**ip summary-address eigrp 100 10.10.0.0 255.255.0.0**	Enables manual summarization on this specific interface for the given address and mask

CAUTION: EIGRP automatically summarizes networks at the classful boundary. A poorly designed network with discontiguous subnets could have problems with connectivity if the summarization feature is left on. You could have two routers advertise the same network—172.16.0.0/16—when in fact the intention is for the routers to advertise two different networks—172.16.10.0/24 and 172.16.20.0/24.

Recommended practice is that you turn off automatic summarization, use the **ip summary-address** command, and summarize manually what you need to.

Verifying EIGRP

Router#**show ip eigrp neighbors**	Displays a neighbor table
Router#**show ip eigrp neighbors detail**	Displays a detailed neighbor table
Router#**show ip eigrp interfaces**	Displays information for each interface
Router#**show ip eigrp int s 0/0**	Displays information for a specific interface
Router#**show ip eigrp int 100**	Displays information for interfaces running process 100
Router#**show ip eigrp topology**	Displays the topology table. This command will show you where your feasible successors are
Router#**show ip eigrp traffic**	Displays the number and type of packets sent and received

Troubleshooting EIGRP

Router#**debug eigrp fsm**	Displays events/actions related to the DUAL FSM
Router#**debug eigrp packet**	Displays events/actions related to EIGRP packets
Router#**debug eigrp neighbor**	Displays events/actions related to EIGRP neighbors

Configuration Example: EIGRP

Figure 10-1 shows the network topology for the configuration that follows, which shows how to configure EIGRP using the commands covered in this chapter.

Figure 10-1   Network Topology for EIGRP Configuration

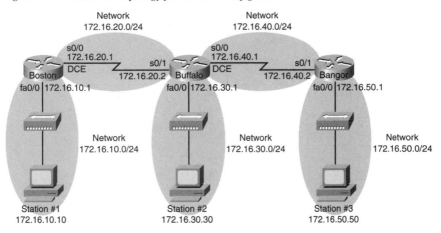

NOTE: The host name, password, and interfaces have all been configured as per the configuration example in Chapter 6, "Configuring a Single Cisco Router."

Boston Router

Boston>**en**	
Boston#**config t**	
Boston(config)#**router eigrp 100**	Enables EIGRP routing

Boston(config-router)#no auto-summary	Disables auto summarization
Boston(config-router)#eigrp log-neighbor-changes	Changes with neighbors will be displayed
Boston(config-router)#network 172.16.0.0	Advertises directly connected networks (classful address only)
Boston(config-router)#exit	
Boston(config)#exit	
Boston#copy run start	

Buffalo Router

Buffalo>en	
Buffalo#config t	
Buffalo(config)#router eigrp 100	Enables EIGRP routing
Buffalo(config-router)#no auto-summary	Disables auto summarization
Buffalo(config-router)#eigrp log-neighbor-changes	Changes with neighbors will be displayed
Buffalo(config-router)#network 172.16.0.0	Advertises directly connected networks (classful address only)
Buffalo(config-router)#Ctrl Z	Exits back to privileged mode
Buffalo#copy run start	

Bangor Router

Bangor>en	
Bangor#config t	

`Bangor(config)#`**`router eigrp 100`**	Enables EIGRP routing
`Bangor(config-router)#`**`no auto-summary`**	Disables auto summarization
`Bangor(config-router)#`**`eigrp log-neighbor-changes`**	Changes with neighbors will be displayed
`Bangor(config-router)#`**`network 172.16.0.0`**	Advertises directly connected networks (classful address only)
`Bangor(config-router)#`Ctrl z	Exits back to privileged mode
`Bangor#`**`copy run start`**	

CHAPTER 11

Single-Area OSPF

This chapter provides information and commands concerning the following Open Shortest Path First (OSPF) topics:

- Configuring single-area OSPF (mandatory commands)
- Using wildcard masks with OSPF areas
- Configuring single-area OSPF (optional commands), regarding
  - Loopback interfaces
  - DR/BDR election priority
  - Cost metrics
  - Authentication
  - Timers
  - Propagating a default route
- Verifying OSPF
- Troubleshooting OSPF

OSPF Routing: Mandatory Commands

Router(config)#router ospf 123 Router(config-router)#	Turns on OSPF process number 123. The process ID is any value between 1–65535. The process ID *is not related to* the OSPF area
Router(config-router)#network 172.16.10.0 0.0.0.255 area 0	OSPF advertises interfaces, not networks. Uses the wildcard mask to determine which interfaces to advertise. Read this line to say: Any interface with an address of 172.16.10.x is to be put into Area 0

NOTE: The process ID number of one router does not have to match the process ID number of any other router. Unlike Interior Gateway Routing Protocol (IGRP) or Enhanced IGRP (EIGRP), matching this number across all routers does *not* ensure network adjacencies will form.

Wildcard Masks

When compared to an IP address, a wildcard mask will identify what addresses get matched for placement into an area:

- A 0 (zero) in a wildcard mask means to check the corresponding bit in the address for an exact match.
- A 1 (one) in a wildcard mask means to ignore the corresponding bit in the address—can be either 1 or 0.

Example 1: 172.16.0.0 0.0.255.255

```
    172.16.0.0  =  10101100.00010000.00000000.00000000
 0.0.255.255  =  00000000.00000000.11111111.11111111
```

```
       Result  =  10101100.00010000.xxxxxxxx.xxxxxxxx
                  172.16.x.x (anything between 172.16.0.0 and 172.16.255.255)
```

TIP: An octet of all zeros means that the address has to match exactly to the address. An octet of all ones means that the address can be ignored.

Example 2: 172.16.8.0 0.0.7.255

```
   172.168.8.0  =  10101100.00010000.00001000.00000000
 0.0.0.7.255  =  00000000.00000000.00000111.11111111
```

```
       Result  =  10101100.00010000.00001xxx.xxxxxxxx
      00001xxx  =  00001000 to 00001111  =  8–15
      xxxxxxxx  =  00000000 to 11111111  =  0–255
                  Anything between 172.16.8.0 and 172.16.15.255
```

Using Wildcard Masks with OSPF Areas

`Router(config-router)#network 172.16.10.1` `0.0.0.0 area 0`	Read this line to say: Any interface with an exact address of 172.16.10.1 is to be put into Area 0
`Router(config-router)#network 172.16.10.0` `0.0.255.255 area 0`	Read this line to say: Any interface with an address of 172.16.x.x is to be put into Area 0
`Router(config-router)#network 0.0.0.0` `255.255.255.255 area 0`	Read this line to say: Any interface with any address is to be put into Area 0

OSPF Routing: Optional Commands

Loopback Interfaces

`Router(config)#interface lo0`	Moves to virtual interface Loopback 0
`Router(config-if)#ip address 192.168.100.1 255.255.255.255`	Assigns IP address to interface

NOTE: Loopback interfaces are always "up and up" and do not go down unless manually shut down. This makes Loopback interfaces great for using as an OSPF router ID.

OSPF DR/BDR Election

`Router(config)#int S0/0`	
`Router(config-if)#ip ospf priority 50`	Changes OSPF interface priority to 50

NOTE: The assigned priority can be between 0 and 255. A priority of 0 guarantees that the router never wins a designated router (DR) election, and 255 guarantees a tie in the election (tie broken by highest router ID). If all routers have the same priority, regardless of the number, they tie. Ties are broken by the highest router ID. Since 255 is the highest possible priority, a router with a priority of 255 is merely guaranteed to be part of a tie-breaker, and will not lose due to higher priority.

Modifying OSPF Cost Metrics

`Router(config)#int s 0/0`	
`Router(config-if)#bandwidth 128`	By changing the bandwidth, OSPF will recalculate cost of link
or	
`Router(config-if)#ip ospf cost 1564`	Changes the cost to a value of 1564

NOTE: The cost of a link is determined by dividing the reference bandwidth by the interface bandwidth.

The default reference bandwidth is 10^8.

Bandwidth is a number between 1–10,000,000 and is measured in kilobits.

Cost is a number between 1–65,535. Cost has no unit of measurement—it is just a number.

TIP: For OSPF to calculate routes properly, all interfaces connected to the same link must agree on the cost of that link. Therefore, if you change the reference bandwidth on one router, you must change it to match on all routers in that area.

OSPF Authentication: Simple

`Router(config)#`**`router ospf 456`**	
`Router(config-router)#`**`area 0 authentication`**	Turns on simple authentication. Password sent in clear text
`Router(config-router)#`**`exit`**	
`Router(config)#`**`int fa 0/0`**	
`Router(config-if)#`**`ip ospf authentication-key fred`**	Sets key (password) to **fred**

OSPF Authentication Using MD5 Encryption

`Router(config)#`**`router ospf 456`**	
`Router(config-router)#`**`area 0 authentication message-digest`**	Enables authentication with MD5 password encryption
`Router(config-router)#`**`exit`**	
`Router(config)#`**`int fa 0/0`**	

Router(config-if)#**ip ospf message-digest-key 1 md5 fred**	**1** is the *key-id*. This value must be the same as that of the neighboring router **md5** indicates that the MD5 hash algorithm will be used **fred** is the key (password) and must be the same as that of the neighboring router

OSPF Timers

Router(config-if)#**ip ospf hello-interval timer 20**	Changes Hello Interval timer to 20 seconds
Router(config-if)#**ip ospf dead-interval 80**	Changes Dead Interval timer to 80 seconds

NOTE: The Hello and Dead Interval timers must match for routers to become neighbors.

Propagating a Default Route

Router(config)#**ip route 0.0.0.0 0.0.0.0 s0/0**	Creates a default route
Router(config)#**router ospf 1**	
Router(config-router)#**default-information-originate**	Sets the default route to be propagated to all OSPF routers

Verifying OSPF Configuration

Router#**show ip protocol**	Displays parameters for all protocols running on router
Router#**show ip route**	Displays complete IP routing table

Router#**show ip ospf**	Displays basic information
Router#**show ip ospf** interface	Displays OSPF information as it relates to all interfaces
Router#**show ip ospf** int fa 0/0	Displays OSPF information for interface fa 0/0
Router#**show ip ospf** neighbor	Lists all OSPF neighbors and their states
Router#**show ip ospf** neighbor detail	Displays a detailed list of neighbors
Router#**show ip ospf** database	Displays contents of OSPF database

Troubleshooting OSPF

Router#**clear ip route** *	Clears entire routing table, forcing it to rebuild
Router#**clear ip route** a.b.c.d	Clears specific route to network a.b.c.d
Router#**clear ip ospf** counters	Resets OSPF counters
Router#**clear ip ospf** process	Resets *entire* OSPF process forcing OSPF to re-create neighbors, database, and routing table
Router#**debug ip ospf** events	Displays *all* OSPF events
Router#**debug ip ospf** adj	Displays various OSPF states and DR and BDR election between adjacent routers
Router#**debug ip ospf** packets	Displays OPSF packets

Configuration Example: Single-Area OSPF

Figure 11-1 shows the network topology for the configuration that follows, which shows a single-area OSPF network configuration using the commands covered in this chapter.

Figure 11-1   Network Topology for Single-Area OSPF Configuration

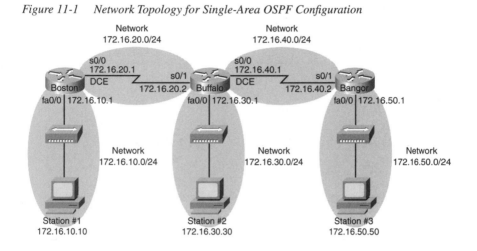

Boston Router

`Router>`**`en`**	
`Router#`**`config t`**	
`Router(config)#`**`no ip domain-lookup`**	Turns off DNS queries so that spelling mistakes will not slow you down
`Router(config)#`**`hostname Boston`**	Sets host name
`Boston(config)#`**`line con 0`**	
`Boston(config-line)#`**`logging sync`**	Commands interrupted by console messages will be appended to a new line
`Boston(config-line)#`**`exit`**	
`Boston(config)#`**`int fa 0/0`**	
`Boston(config-if)#`**`ip add 172.16.10.1 255.255.255.0`**	
`Boston(config-if)#`**`no shut`**	

`Boston(config-if)#int s0/0`	
`Boston(config-if)#ip add 172.16.20.1` `255.255.255.0`	
`Boston(config-if)#clock rate 56000`	DCE cable connected to this interface
`Boston(config-if)#no shut`	
`Boston(config-if)#exit`	
`Boston(config)#router ospf 1`	Turns on OSPF process 1
`Boston(config-router)#net 172.16.10.0 0.0.0.255` `area 0`	Any interface with address of 172.10.10.x will be part of Area 0
`Boston(config-router)#net 172.16.20.0 0.0.0.255` `area 0`	Any interface with address of 172.16.20.x will be part of Area 0
`Boston(config-router)#`Ctrl z	
`Boston#copy run start`	

Buffalo Router

`Router>en`	
`Router#config t`	
`Router(config)#no ip domain-lookup`	Turns off DNS queries so that spelling mistakes will not slow you down
`Router(config)#hostname Buffalo`	Sets host name
`Buffalo(config)#line con 0`	
`Buffalo(config-line)#logging sync`	Commands interrupted by console messages will be appended to a new line

Buffalo(config-line)#**exit**	
Buffalo(config)#**int fa 0/0**	
Buffalo(config-if)#**ip add 172.16.30.1 255.255.255.0**	
Buffalo(config-if)#**no shut**	
Buffalo(config-if)#**int s0/0**	
Buffalo(config-if)#**ip add 172.16.40.1 255.255.255.0**	
Buffalo(config-if)#**clock rate 56000**	DCE cable connected to this interface
Buffalo(config-if)#**no shut**	
Buffalo(config)#**int s 0/1**	
Buffalo(config-if)#**ip add 172.16.20.2 255.255.255.0**	
Buffalo(config-if)#**no shut**	
Buffalo(config-if)#**exit**	
Buffalo(config)#**router ospf 463**	Turns on OSPF process 463
Buffalo(config-router)#**net 172.16.0.0 0.0.255.255 area 0**	Any interface with address of 172.16.x.x will be part of Area 0
Buffalo(config-router)#Ctrl Z	
Buffalo#**copy run start**	

Bangor Router

Router>**en**	
Router#**config t**	
Router(config)#**no ip domain-lookup**	Turns off DNS queries so that spelling mistakes will not slow you down

Router(config)#**hostname Buffalo**	Sets host name
Bangor(config)#**line con 0**	
Bangor(config-line)#**logging sync**	Commands interrupted by console messages will be appended to a new line
Bangor(config-line)#**exit**	
Bangor(config)#**int fa 0/0**	
Bangor(config-if)#**ip add 172.16.50.1 255.255.255.0**	
Bangor(config-if)#**no shut**	
Bangor(config)#**int s 0/1**	
Bangor(config-if)#**ip add 172.16.40.2 255.255.255.0**	
Bangor(config-if)#**no shut**	
Bangor(config-if)#**exit**	
Bangor(config)#**router ospf 100**	Turns on OSPF process 100
Bangor(config-router)#**net 172.16.40.2 0.0.0.0 area 0**	Interface with address of 172.16.40.2 will be part of Area 0
Bangor(config-router)#**net 172.16.50.1 0.0.0.0 area 0**	Interface with address of 172.16.50.1 will be part of Area 0
Bangor(config-router)#Ctrl z	
Bangor#**copy run start**	

PART V

Switches

Chapter 12   Configuring a Switch

Chapter 13   Spanning Tree Protocol and EtherChannel

Chapter 14   VLANs

Chapter 15   VTP and Inter-VLAN Communication

Configuring a Switch

This chapter provides information and commands concerning the following topics:

*   Configuring a switch (1900/2900/2950 Series), including
    —   Host names
    —   Passwords
    —   IP addresses and default gateways
    —   Interface descriptions
    —   Duplex and speed settings
    —   Working with the MAC address table
    —   Port security
*   Resetting switch configurations (1900/2900/2950 series)

> **TIP:** The 1900 series switch uses an interactive menu system. Selecting different letters from the menu will take you to different places in the operating system. For this book, and for better control of the 1900 series switch, select the command-line option by pressing the letter Ⓚ to get to the user mode prompt >.

Help Commands

`switch>?`	The **?** works here the same as in a router

Command Modes

`switch>`**enable**	User mode, same as a router
`switch#`	Privileged mode
`switch#`**disable**	Leaves privileged mode
`switch>`**exit**	Leaves user mode

Verifying Commands

switch#**show version**	Displays information on software and hardware
switch#**show flash:**	Displays information on Flash memory (for the 2900/2950 series only)
switch#**show mac-address-table**	Displays current MAC address forwarding table
switch#**show controllers ethernet-controller**	Displays information about Ethernet controller
switch#**show running-config**	Displays current configuration in DRAM
switch#**show start**	Displays current configuration in NVRAM
switch#**show post**	Displays whether the switch passed POST
switch#**show vlan**	Displays the current VLAN configuration
switch#**show interfaces**	Displays interface configuration and status of line: up/up, up/down, admin down
switch#**show interface vlan1**	Displays setting of virtual interface VLAN 1, the default VLAN on the switch

Resetting Switch Configuration

1900 Series Switch

1900switch#**delete vtp**	Removes VLAN Trunking Protocol (VTP) information
1900switch#**delete nvram**	Resets switch back to factory defaults
1900switch>**en**	
1900switch#**reload**	Restarts the switch

2900/2950 Series Switch

`switch#`**`delete flash:vlan.dat`**	Removes VLAN database from Flash memory
`Delete filename [vlan.dat]?`	Press ⏎**Enter**
`Delete flash:vlan.dat? [confirm]`	Reconfirm by pressing ⏎**Enter**
`Switch#`**`erase startup-config`**	Erases file from NVRAM
`<output omitted>`	
`Switch#`**`reload`**	Restarts the switch

Setting Host Names

1900 Series Switch

`#`**`config t`**	
`(config)#`**`hostname 1900Switch`**	Same method as the router
`1900Switch(config)#`	

2900/2950 Series Switch

`Switch#`**`config t`**	
`Switch(config)#`**`hostname 2900Switch`**	Same method as the router
`2900Switch(config)#`	

Setting Passwords: 1900 Series Switches

`1900Switch(config)#`**`enable password level 1 cisco`**	Sets the user mode password to **cisco**
`1900Switch(config)#`**`enable password level 15 class`**	Sets the enable mode password to **class**
`1900Switch(config)#`**`enable secret scott`**	Sets the enable secret password to **scott**

TIP: The user mode password is what you need to enter to move from the menu system to the CLI. The enable mode password is what you use to move from user mode to privileged mode.

Setting Passwords: 2900/2950 Series Switches

Setting passwords for the 2900/2950 series switches is the same method as used for a router.

2900Switch(config)#**enable password cisco**	Sets enable password to **cisco**
2900Switch(config)#**enable secret class**	Sets encrypted secret password to **class**
2900Switch(config)#**line con 0**	Enters line console mode
2900Switch(config-line)#**login**	Enables password checking
2900Switch(config-line)#**password cisco**	Sets password to **cisco**
2900Switch(config-line)#**exit**	Exits line console mode
2900Switch(config-line)#**line aux 0**	Enters line auxiliary mode
2900Switch(config-line)#**login**	Enables password checking
2900Switch(config-line)#**password cisco**	Sets password to **cisco**
2900Switch(config-line)#**exit**	Exits line auxiliary mode
2900Switch(config-line)#**line vty 0 4**	Enters line vty mode for all five virtual ports
2900Switch(config-line)#**login**	Enables password checking
2900Switch(config-line)#**password cisco**	Sets password to **cisco**
2900Switch(config-line)#**exit**	Exits line vty mode
2900Switch(config)#	

Setting IP Address and Default Gateway

1900 Series Switch

1900Switch(config)#**ip address 172.16.10.2 255.255.255.0**	Sets the IP address and mask to allow for remote access to the switch

1900Switch(config)#**ip default-gateway 172.16.10.1**	Sets the default gateway address to allow IP information an exit past the local network
1900Switch(config)#	

2900/2950 Series Switch

2900Switch(config)#**int vlan1**	Enters virtual interface for VLAN 1, the default VLAN on the switch
2900Switch(config-if)#**ip address 172.16.10.2 255.255.255.0**	Sets the IP address and mask to allow for remote access to the switch
2900Switch(config-if)#**exit**	
2900Switch(config)#**ip default-gateway 172.16.10.1**	To allow IP information an exit past the local network

TIP: For the 2900/2950 series switches, the IP address of the switch is just that—the IP address for the *entire* switch. That is why you set the address in VLAN 1—the default VLAN of the switch—and not in a specific Ethernet interface.

Setting Interface Descriptions

1900 Series Switch

1900Switch(config-if)#**description Finance VLAN**	Adds description of interface

2900/2950 Series Switch

2900Switch(config)#**int fa0/1**	Enters interface mode
2900Switch(config-if)#**description Finance VLAN**	Adds description of interface

TIP: The 1900 series switch has either 12 or 24 Ethernet ports named e0/1, e0/2, ...e0/24. There is also an Ethernet port named e0/25 that is in the back of the switch using an AUI interface. Ports A and B on the front of the switch are named fa0/26 and fa0/27, respectively, regardless of the switch is a 12-port or 24-port model. Ports A and B are Fast Ethernet.

TIP: The 2900 and 2950 series switches have either 12 or 24 Fast Ethernet ports named fa0/1, fa0/2, ...fa0/24.

Setting Duplex Settings: 1900 or 2900/2950 Series Switches

`1900Switch(config)#int e0/1`	Use e0/1 on 2900/2950
`1900Switch(config-if)#duplex full`	Forces full-duplex operation
`1900Switch(config-if)#duplex auto`	Enables auto-duplex config
`1900Switch(config-if)#duplex half`	Forces half-duplex operation

Setting Speed Settings: 2900/2950 Series Switches

`2900Switch(config)#int fa0/1`	
`2900Switch(config-if)#speed 10`	Forces 10-Mbps operation
`2900Switch(config-if)#speed 100`	Forces 100-Mbps operation
`2900Switch(config-if)#speed auto`	Enables autospeed configuration

Setting Web-Based Interface for Configuration: 1900 and 2900/2950 Series Switches

`X900Switch(config)#ip http server`	Turns on HTTP service
`X900Switch(config)#ip http port 80`	Sets port number for HTTP. This port should be turned off for security reasons unless it is being used

Managing the MAC Address Table: 1900 and 2900/2950 Series Switches

switch#**show mac-address-table**	Displays current MAC address forwarding table
switch#**clear mac-address-table**	Deletes all entries from current MAC address forwarding table
switch#**clear mac-address-table dynamic**	Deletes only dynamic entries from table

Configuring Static MAC Addresses

1900 Series Switch

1900Switch(config)#**mac-address-table permanent** *aaaa.aaaa.aaaa* **e0/1**	Sets a permanent address of *aaaa.aaaa.aaaa* in the MAC address table for interface e0/1
1900switch#**clear mac-address-table perm**	Deletes all permanent entries

2900/2950 Series Switch

2900Switch(config)#**mac-address-table static** *aaaa.aaaa.aaaa* **fa0/1 vlan 1**	Sets a permanent address to fa0/1 in VLAN 1
2900Switch(config)#**no mac-address-table static** *aaaa.aaaa.aaaa* **fa0/1 vlan 1**	Removes permanent address to fa0/1 in VLAN 1

Port Security: 1900 Series Switches

1900 Series Switch

1900Switch(config-if)#**port secure**	Interface will become secure
1900Switch(config-if)#**port secure max-mac-count 1**	Only one MAC address will be allowed in the MAC table for this interface

2900 Series Switch

2900Switch(config)#int fa0/1	
2900Switch(config-if)#port security	
2900Switch(config-if)#port security max-mac-count 1	Only one MAC address will be allowed for this interface
2900Switch(config-if)#port security action shutdown	Port will shut down if violation occurs

2950 Series Switch

2950Switch(config)#int fa 0/1	
2950Switch(config-if)#switchport port-security	
2950Switch(config-if)#switchport port-security mac-address sticky	Interface converts all MAC addresses to sticky secure addresses—only the MAC address learned first will now be accepted on this port
2950Switch(config-if)#switchport port-security maximum 1	Only one MAC address will be allowed for this interface
2950Switch(config-if)#switchport port-security violation shutdown	Port will shut down if violation occurs

Verifying Port Security

1900 Series Switch

1900Switch#show mac-address-table security	Displays the MAC address table with security information

2900/2950 Series Switch

2900Switch#show port security	Displays the MAC address table with security information

Configuration Example: 2900 Series Switch

Figure 12-1 shows the network topology for the basic configuration of a 2900 series switch using the commands covered in this chapter.

Figure 12-1   Network Topology for 2900 Series Switch Configuration

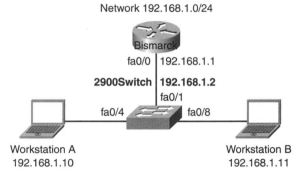

`switch>`**`en`**	Enters privileged mode
`switch#`**`config t`**	Enters global config mode
`switch(config)#`**`no ip domain-lookup`**	Turns off DNS queries so that spelling mistakes will not slow you down
`switch(config)#`**`hostname 2900`**	Sets host name
`2900(config)#`**`enable secret cisco`**	Sets encrypted secret password to **cisco**
`2900(config)#`**`line con 0`**	Enters line console mode
`2900(config-line)#`**`logging synchronous`**	Appends commands to new line; router information will not interrupt
`2900(config-line)#`**`login`**	User must log in to console before use
`2900(config-line)#`**`password switch`**	Sets password to **switch**
`2900(config-line)#`**`exec-timeout 0 0`**	Console will never log out
`2900(config-line)#`**`exit`**	Moves back to global config mode

`2900(config)#line aux 0`	Moves to line auxiliary mode
`2900(config-line)#login`	User must log in to auxiliary port before use
`2900(config-line)#password class`	Sets password to **class**
`2900(config-line)#exit`	Back to global config mode
`2900(config)#line vty 0 15`	Moves to configure all 16 vty ports at same time
`2900(config-line)#login`	User must log in to vty port before use
`2900(config-line)#password class`	Sets password to **class**
`2900(config-line)#exit`	Back to global config mode
`2900(config)#ip default-gateway 192.168.1.1`	Sets default gateway
`2900(config)#int vlan 1`	Moves to virtual interface VLAN 1
`2900(config-if)#ip add 192.168.1.2` `255.255.255.0`	Sets IP address for switch
`2900(config-if)#no shut`	Turns virtual interface on
`2900(config-if)#int fa 0/1`	Moves to interface fa 0/1
`2900(config-if)#desc Link to Router`	Sets local description
`2900(config-if)#int fa 0/4`	Moves to interface fa 0/4
`2900(config-if)#desc Link to Workstation A`	Sets local description
`2900(config-if)#port security`	Activates port security
`2900(config-if)#port security max-mac-count 1`	Only one MAC address will be allowed in the MAC table
`2900(config-if)#port security action shutdown`	Port will be turned off if more than one MAC address is reported
`2900(config-if)#int fa 0/8`	Moves to interface fa 0/8
`2900(config-if)#desc Link to Workstation B`	Sets local description
`2900(config-if)#port security`	Activates port security

`2900(config-if)#`**`port security max-mac-count 1`**	Only one MAC address will be allowed in the MAC table
`2900(config-if)#`**`port security action shutdown`**	Port will be turned off if more than one MAC address is reported
`2900(config-if)#`**`exit`**	Returns to global config mode
`2900(config)#`**`exit`**	Returns to privileged mode
`2900#`**`copy run start`**	Saved configuration to NVRAM
`2900#`	

CHAPTER 13

Spanning Tree Protocol and EtherChannel

This chapter provides information and commands concerning the following topics:

- Spanning-tree verification and troubleshooting
- Change spanning-tree priority of a switch (version 12.0 and 12.1 of IOS)
- Changing the cost of spanning tree on an interface
- Changing the state of spanning tree on an interface
- Spanning Tree Portfast BPDU Guard
- EtherChannel configuration
- Verification of EtherChannel
- EtherChannel tips

Spanning Tree Protocol

Spanning-Tree Verification

Cisco IOS Software Release 12.0	2900#`show spanning-tree brief`	Displays the spanning-tree table of the switch
Cisco IOS Software Release 12.1	Switch#`show spanning-tree`	Displays the spanning-tree table of the switch
	2950#`show spanning-tree int fa 0/17`	Displays spanning-tree info for port fa 0/17
	2950#`show spanning-tree vlan` *x*	Displays spanning-tree info for the specific VLAN
	2950#`debug spanning-tree {all}`	Displays all informational messages about changes in the spanning-tree topology

Change Spanning-Tree Priority of a Switch

Cisco IOS Software Release 12.0	Switch(config)#**spanning-tree priority 1**	Number can be from 1–65535. Lower number means better chance of being elected the root bridge. The default is 32768
Cisco IOS Software Release 12.1	Switch(config)#**spanning-tree vlan 1 priority 1**	Number can be from 1–65535. Lower number means better chance of being elected the root bridge. The default is 32768
	Switch#**spanning-tree vlan** x **root**	Changes this switch to the root switch for VLAN x by lowering its priority to either 24576 or 100 less than current root bridge, whichever number is lower

Changing the Cost of Spanning Tree on an Interface

Switch#**config t**	
Switch(config)#**int fa 0/1**	
Switch(config-if)#**spanning-tree cost** x	Sets spanning-tree cost to specified value of x

Changing the State of Spanning Tree on an Interface

Switch(config)#**int fa 0/1**	
Switch(config-if)#**spanning-tree portfast**	See the Caution that follows

CAUTION: The command **spanning-tree portfast** will force a port to move directly to the Forwarding state, without having to transition through the Blocking, Listening, and Learning states.

This can save up to 50 seconds of wait time. This is an excellent command on access ports that will never be hooked up to another switch. Examples where this would be useful are on ports connected to computers or other end devices, such as printers, servers, and so on. You must exercise caution with this command, however, because if a switch port is plugged into another switch and the **portfast** command is enabled, then spanning tree will be defeated and a potential switching loop might be created.

Spanning Tree Portfast BPDU Guard Command

Switch#`config t`	
Switch(config)#`spanning-tree portfast bpduguard`	Enables BPDU Guard for all interfaces
Switch(config)#`errdisable recovery cause bpduguard`	Allows port to re-enable itself by setting a recovery timer
Switch(config)#`errdisable recovery interval 400`	Sets recovery timer to 400 seconds. Default is 300 seconds
Switch(config)#`show spanning-tree summary totals`	Verifies if BPDU Guard is enabled or disabled
Switch#`show errdisable recovery`	Displays errdisable recovery timer information

NOTE: There is a feature that has been added to Catalyst IOS called *Spanning Tree Portfast BPDU Guard*. This feature has been created to maintain stability within the active STP topology. Devices that are attached to ports with Portfast enabled are not allowed to take part in the spanning-tree process. If a port that has Portfast enabled receives a BPDU packet, that port is disabled by the switch. This is done by transitioning the port into the *errdisable* state. An error message will be sent to the console. Ports disabled by STP BPDU Guard remain in the disabled state unless it is manually enabled with the **no shut** command or configured to re-enable itself automatically.

EtherChannel

EtherChannel Configuration

Switch#`config t`	
Switch(config)#`int fa 0/11`	
Switch(config-if)#`channel-group x mode on`	x is the number of the channel-group and must match the other interface
Switch(config-if)#`int fa 0/12`	
Switch(config-if)#`channel-group x mode on`	x is the number of the channel-group and must match the other interface

Verification of EtherChannel

`Switch#show etherchannel x detail`	Displays detailed information
`Switch#show etherchannel x port`	Displays EtherChannel port information
`Switch#show etherchannel x port-channel`	Displays port-channel information
`Switch#show etherchannel x summary`	Displays a one-line summary per channel-group

EtherChannel Tips

- Can combine from two to eight parallel Ethernet links
- 1900 Switches need 8.00.03 or later Enterprise Edition software
- 2900 Switches need IOS 11.2(8)SA or later
- 2950 Switches need IOS 12.0(5.2)WC(1) or later
- There are three different modes for EtherChannel—**auto**, **desirable**, and **on**:
  - **auto** tells switch to wait for other switch to start EtherChannel negotiations. If **auto** is set on both sides, EtherChannel will never form—both sides are waiting for the other side to start negotiating!
  - **desirable** tells switch it is willing to turn EtherChannel on.
  - **on** tells switch it wants to form an EtherChannel.

  Only the combinations of **auto-desirable**, **desirable-desirable**, and **on-on** will allow a channel to be formed.

  If a device on one side of the channel does not support PAgP, such as a router, the device on the other side must have PAgP set to **on**.
- All ports must be identical
  - Same Speed and Duplex
- Cannot mix Fast Ethernet and Gigabit Ethernet
- Must all be VLAN trunk or non-trunk operational status

CHAPTER 14

VLANs

This chapter provides information and commands concerning the following topics for 1900, 2900, and 2950 series switches:

- Displaying VLAN information
- Creating static VLANs
- Assigning ports to VLANs
- Assigning ports using the **range** command (2950 series switch only)
- Saving VLAN configurations
- Erasing VLAN configurations
- Troubleshooting VLANs

Displaying VLAN Information

1900 Series Switch

1900Switch#**show vlan**	Shows VLAN information
1900Switch#**show vlan-membership**	Shows which ports belong to which VLAN
1900Switch#**show vlan 2**	Displays information about VLAN 2 only

2900/2950 Series Switch

2900Switch#**show vlan**	Shows all VLAN status
2900Switch#**show vlan brief**	Shows all VLAN status in brief
2900Switch#**show vlan id 2**	Displays information of VLAN 2 only
2900Switch#**show vlan name Marketing**	Displays information of VLAN named Marketing only

Creating Static VLANs

1900 Series Switch

1900Switch#**config t**	
1900Switch(config)#**vlan 2 name Engineering**	Creates VLAN 2 and names it Engineering
1900Switch(config)#**vlan 3 name Marketing**	Creates VLAN 3 and names it Marketing

2900 Series Switch

2900Switch#**vlan database**	Enters VLAN database mode
2900(vlan)#**vlan 2 name Engineering**	Creates VLAN 2 and names it Engineering
2900(vlan)#**vlan 3 name Marketing**	Creates VLAN 3 and names it Marketing
2900(vlan)#**exit**	Applies changes and exits VLAN database mode
2900#	

2950 Series Switch

2950Switch#**config t**	Enters global config mode
2950Switch(config)#**vlan 10**	Creates VLAN 10 and enters VLAN config mode for further definitions
2950Switch(config-vlan)#**name Accounting**	Assigns a name to a VLAN
2950Switch(config-vlan)#**exit**	Moves back to global config mode
2950Switch(config)#**vlan 20**	Creates VLAN 20 and enters VLAN config mode for further definitions
2950Switch(config-vlan)#**name Sales**	Assigns a name to a VLAN
2950Switch(config-vlan)#**exit**	Moves back to global config mode

TIP: For the 2900 series switch, you must apply the changes to the VLAN database for the changes to take effect. You can also use the command **apply** in the VLAN database, which will apply the changes, but not exit the mode. Using the Ctrl z command to exit out of the VLAN database will not apply the changes to the VLAN database. You must use the command **exit** to exit the VLAN database and have the changes successfully applied.

TIP: For the 2950 series switch, the use of the VLAN database is being phased out, in favor of creating VLANs in the manner demonstrated in the preceding command syntax. If you use the **vlan database** command at the 2950Switch# prompt, the 2950 IOS will tell you this but will still allow you to use commands the same as the 2900 series switch. Get used to this style; it is the method to be used on all future releases of switches.

Assigning Ports to VLANs

1900 Series Switch

1900Switch#**config t**	
1900Switch(config)#**int e0/2**	Moves to interface mode
1900Switch(config-if)#**vlan static 2**	Assigns this port to VLAN 2
1900Switch(config-if)#**int e0/3**	Moves to interface mode
1900Switch(config-if)#**vlan static 3**	Assigns this port to VLAN 3
1900Switch(config-if)#**exit**	Exits interface mode
1900Switch(config)#	

2900/2950 Series Switch

2900Switch#**config t**	
2900Switch(config)#**int fa0/2**	Moves to interface mode
2900Switch(config-if)#**switchport mode access**	Sets switchport mode to access
2900Switch(config-if)#**switchport access vlan 2**	Assigns this port to VLAN 2
2900Switch(config-if)#**int fa0/3**	Moves to interface mode

`2900Switch(config-if)#`**`switchport mode access`**	Sets switchport mode to access
`2900Switch(config-if)#`**`switchport access vlan 3`**	Assigns this port to VLAN 3
`2900Switch(config-if)#`**`exit`**	Exits interface mode
`2900Switch(config)#`	

Assigning Ports Using the range Command (2950 Switch Only)

`2950Switch(config)#`**`int range fa 0/1 - 4`**	Enables you to set the same configuration parameters on multiple ports at the same time. Note that there is a space before and after the hyphen
`2950Switch(config-if-range)#`**`switchport mode access`**	Sets all ports to access mode
`2950Switch(config-if-range)#`**`switchport access vlan 10`**	Assigns all ports to VLAN 10

Saving VLAN Configurations

1900 Series Switch

Any command made to a 1900 series switch is automatically saved to NVRAM. There is no **copy run start** command on a 1900 series switch.

2900/2950 Series Switch

Any command entered in the VLAN database is automatically saved as long as you leave the VLAN database properly with the **exit** command, and not Ctrl z.

`Switch#`**`copy run start`**	Saves the running-config to NVRAM

Erasing VLAN Configurations

1900 Series Switch

1900Switch#**delete vtp**	Deletes all VLAN information from the switch and resets VTP parameters to the factory defaults
or	
1900Switch(config)#**int fa 0/2**	
1900Switch(config-if)#**no vlan static 2**	Removes interface from VLAN 2 and puts it back into default VLAN 1
1900Switch(config-if)#**exit**	
1900Switch(config)#**no vlan 2 name Engineering**	Removes only VLAN 2 from database
1900Switch(config)#	

2900/2950 Series Switch

2900Switch#**delete flash:vlan.dat**	Removes entire VLAN database from Flash memory Make sure there is *no* space between the colon (:) and the characters **vlan.dat**. You can potentially erase the entire contents of Flash memory with this command if the syntax is not correct
2900Switch#**delete flash:**	
Delete filename [ ]? **vlan.dat**	Removes entire VLAN database from Flash memory
Delete flash:vlan.dat? [confirm]	Press the ⏎Enter key
2900Switch#	

or	
2900Switch#**config t**	
2900Switch(config)#**int fa 0/3**	
2900Switch(config-if)#**no switchport access vlan 3**	Removes port from VLAN 3 and reassigns it to default VLAN 1
2900Switch(config-if)#**exit**	
2900Switch(config)#**exit**	
2900Switch#**vlan database**	Enters VLAN database mode
2900(vlan)#**no vlan 3**	Removes only VLAN 2 from database
2900(vlan)#**exit**	Applies changes and exits VLAN database mode

NOTE: For the 1900 series switch, removing a VLAN from the database *does not* reassign ports in that VLAN back to the default Management VLAN. You must also go into the specific interface and reassign the ports as well.

NOTE: For any series switch, you cannot remove VLAN 1.

Troubleshooting VLANs

2900Switch#**show vlan**	Displays the complete VLAN database
2900Switch#**show vlan brief**	Displays a summary of the VLAN database
2900Switch#**show interfaces**	Displays a summary of each interface, including speed and duplex settings
2900Switch#**debug sw-vlan packets**	Displays information about VLAN packets a router has received but is not capable of supporting

Configuration Example: 2900 Switch Configuration

Figure 14-1 shows the network topology for the configuration of VLANs on a 2900 series switch using the commands covered in this chapter.

Figure 14-1   Network Topology for VLAN Configuration on a 2900 Series Switch

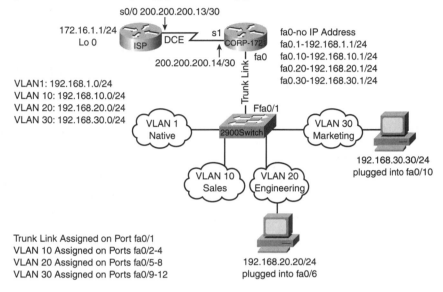

NOTE: This example shows the configuration of the switch only. Chapter 15, "VTP and Inter-VLAN Communication," covers configuration of the routers.

`switch>`**`en`**	Enters privileged mode
`switch#`**`config t`**	Enters global configuration mode
`switch(config)#`**`hostname 2900Switch`**	Sets the host name
`2900Switch(config)#`**`no ip domain-lookup`**	Turns off checking for DNS entries on spelling mistakes
`2900Switch(config)#`**`enable secret cisco`**	Sets the secret password to **cisco**
`2900Switch(config)#`**`line con 0`**	Enters console mode

`2900Switch(config-line)#`**`logging synchronous`**	Informational lines will not affect the command being entered
`2900Switch(config-line)#`**`login`**	Turns on password challenge for console mode
`2900Switch(config-line)#`**`password class`**	Sets password to **class**
`2900Switch(config-line)#`**`exit`**	Returns to global config mode
`2900Switch(config)#`**`line vty 0 15`**	Enters all 16 vty modes. The same commands will apply to all lines
`2900Switch(config-line)#`**`login`**	Challenges a remote user for a password
`2900Switch(config-line)#`**`password  class`**	Sets the password to **class**
`2900Switch(config-line)#`**`exit`**	Returns to global config mode
`2900Switch(config)#`**`ip default-gateway 192.168.1.1`**	Sets the default gateway for switch
`2900Switch(config)#`**`int vlan1`**	Enters the virtual interface VLAN 1
`2900Switch(config-if)#`**`ip address 192.168.1.2 255.255.255.0`**	Sets the IP address of the switch
`2900Switch(config-if)#`**`no shut`**	Turns on the interface
`2900Switch(config-if)#`**`exit`**	Returns to global config mode
`2900Switch(config)#`**`exit`**	Returns to privileged mode
`2900Switch#`**`vlan database`**	Enters the VLAN database
`2900Switch(vlan)#`**`vlan 10 name Sales`**	Creates VLAN 10
`2900Switch(vlan)#`**`vlan 20 name Engineering`**	Creates VLAN 20
`2900Switch(vlan)#`**`vlan 30 name Marketing`**	Creates VLAN 30
`2900Switch(vlan)#`**`exit`**	Applies VLAN information and exits
`2900Switch#`**`config t`**	Enters global configuration mode

`2900Switch(config)#`**`int fa0/2`**	Moves to interface mode
`2900Switch(config-if)#`**`switchport mode access`**	Sets the switchport mode to access
`2900Switch(config-if)#`**`switchport access vlan 10`**	Assigns this port to VLAN 10
`2900Switch(config-if)#`**`int fa0/3`**	Moves to interface mode
`2900Switch(config-if)#`**`switchport mode access`**	Sets the switchport mode to access
`2900Switch(config-if)#`**`switchport access vlan 10`**	Assigns this port to VLAN 10
`2900Switch(config)#`**`int fa0/4`**	Moves to interface mode
`2900Switch(config-if)#`**`switchport mode access`**	Sets the switchport mode to access
`2900Switch(config-if)#`**`switchport access vlan 10`**	Assigns this port to VLAN 10
`2900Switch(config-if)#`**`int fa0/5`**	Moves to interface mode
`2900Switch(config-if)#`**`switchport mode access`**	Sets the switchport mode to access
`2900Switch(config-if)#`**`switchport access vlan 20`**	Assigns this port to VLAN 20
`2900Switch(config)#`**`int fa0/6`**	Moves to interface mode
`2900Switch(config-if)#`**`switchport mode access`**	Sets the switchport mode to access
`2900Switch(config-if)#`**`switchport access vlan 20`**	Assigns this port to VLAN 20
`2900Switch(config-if)#`**`int fa0/7`**	Moves to interface mode
`2900Switch(config-if)#`**`switchport mode access`**	Sets the switchport mode to access
`2900Switch(config-if)#`**`switchport access vlan 20`**	Assigns this port to VLAN 20
`2900Switch(config)#`**`int fa0/8`**	Moves to interface mode
`2900Switch(config-if)#`**`switchport mode access`**	Sets the switchport mode to access
`2900Switch(config-if)#`**`switchport access vlan 20`**	Assigns this port to VLAN 20
`2900Switch(config-if)#`**`int fa0/9`**	Moves to interface mode

`2900Switch(config-if)#`**`switchport mode access`**	Sets the switchport mode to access
`2900Switch(config-if)#`**`switchport access vlan 30`**	Assigns this port to VLAN 30
`2900Switch(config)#`**`int fa0/10`**	Moves to interface mode
`2900Switch(config-if)#`**`switchport mode access`**	Sets the switchport mode to access
`2900Switch(config-if)#`**`switchport access vlan 30`**	Assigns this port to VLAN 30
`2900Switch(config-if)#`**`int fa0/11`**	Moves to interface mode
`2900Switch(config-if)#`**`switchport mode access`**	Sets the switchport mode to access
`2900Switch(config-if)#`**`switchport access vlan 30`**	Assigns this port to VLAN 30
`2900Switch(config)#`**`int fa0/12`**	Moves to interface mode
`2900Switch(config-if)#`**`switchport mode access`**	Sets the switchport mode to access
`2900Switch(config-if)#`**`switchport access vlan 30`**	Assigns this port to VLAN 30
`2900Switch(config-if)#`Ctrl z	Returns to privileged mode
`2900Switch#`**`copy run start`**	Saves config to NVRAM

CHAPTER 15

VTP and Inter-VLAN Communication

This chapter provides information and commands concerning the following topics for 1900, 2900, and 2950 series switches:

- Configuring ISL trunks
- Configuring Dot1Q trunks
- Verifying trunking
- VTP configuration
- Confirming VTP configuration
- Inter-VLAN communication: Router-on-a-stick
- Router-on-a-stick tips

Configuring ISL Trunks

NOTE: The 1900 series switch supports only Inter-Switch Link (ISL) trunking. The 2900 series switch supports both ISL and Dot1Q trunking. The 2950 series switch supports only Dot1Q trunking.

1900 Series Switch

1900Switch(config)#int fa 0/26	Enters interface mode
1900Switch(config-if)#trunk on	Turns trunking mode on

2900 Series Switch

2900Switch(config)#int fa 0/1	Enters interface mode
2900Switch(config-if)#switchport mode trunk	Turns port to trunking mode
2900Switch(config-if)#switchport trunk encapsulation isl	Sets encapsulation type to ISL

NOTE: Trunking can only occur on a Fast Ethernet port. A 1900 series switch has only two Fast Ethernet ports—ports A and B. These are defined as fa 0/26 and FA 0/27 in the command-line interface (CLI).

NOTE: For any series switch, you must set trunk mode at both ends of the link for the trunk to become active.

Configuring Dot1Q Trunks

2900 Series Switch

2900Switch(config)#**int fa 0/1**	Enters interface mode
2900Switch(config-if)#**switchport mode trunk**	Turns port to trunking mode
2900Switch(config-if)#**switchport trunk encapsulation dot1q**	Sets encapsulation type to Dot1Q—this is the default encapsulation type

2950 Series Switch

2950Switch(config)#**int fa 0/1**	Enters interface mode
2950Switch(config-if)#**switchport mode trunk**	Turns port to trunking mode

Verifying Trunking

1900 Series Switch

1900Switch#**show trunk A**	Displays trunking information about port 0/26
DISL state: On, Trunking: On, Encapsulation type: ISL 1900Switch#	

2900 and 2950 Series Switches

29x0Switch#**show int fa 0/1 switchport** Name: Fa0/1 Switchport: Enabled Administrative mode: trunk Operational Mode: trunk Administrative Trunking Encapsulation: isl Operational Trunking Encapsulation: isl <output cut> 29x0Switch#	Shows the status of the interface, including trunking information

VTP Configuration

1900 Series Switch

`1900Switch(config)#`**`vtp client`**	Changes the switch to VTP client mode
`1900Switch(config)#`**`vtp server`**	Changes the switch to default VTP server mode
`1900Switch(config)#`**`vtp transparent`**	Changes the switch to VTP transparent mode
`1900Switch(config)#`**`vtp domain CNAP`**	Sets the name of the VTP management domain to CNAP
`1900Switch(config)#`**`vtp password cisco`**	Sets the VTP password to **cisco**

2900 Series Switch

`2900Switch#`**`vlan database`**	Enters VLAN database mode
`2900Switch(vlan)#`**`vtp client`**	Changes the switch to client mode
`2900Switch(vlan)#`**`vtp server`**	Changes the switch to server mode
`2900Switch(vlan)#`**`vtp transparent`**	Changes the switch to transparent mode
`2900Switch(vlan)#`**`vtp domain academy`**	Sets the name of the VTP management domain to academy
`2900Switch(vlan)#`**`vtp password catalyst`**	Sets the VTP password to **catalyst**
`2900Switch(vlan)#`**`vtp v2-mode`**	Sets VTP mode to version 2
`2900Switch(vlan)#`**`vtp pruning`**	Enables VTP pruning
`2900Switch(vlan)#`**`exit`**	Applies the changes and exits mode
`2900Switch#`	

2950 Series Switch

`2950Switch#`**`config t`**	Enters global config mode
`2950Switch(config)#`**`vtp mode client`**	Changes the switch to client mode
`2950Switch(config)#`**`vtp mode server`**	Changes the switch to server mode

2950Switch(config)#**vtp mode transparent**	Changes the switch to transparent mode
2950Switch(config)#**vtp domain academy**	Sets the name of the VTP management domain to academy
2950Switch(config)#**vtp password catalyst**	Sets the VTP password to catalyst
2950Switch(config)#**vtp v2-mode**	Sets VTP mode to version 2
2950Switch(config)#**vtp pruning**	Enables VTP pruning

NOTE: VTP versions 1 and 2 are not interoperable. All switches must use the same version. The biggest difference between version 1 and 2 is that version 2 has support for Token Ring VLANs.

CAUTION: Switches that are in client mode update their VLAN database from switches that are in server mode. If you have two or more switches intercon-nected and you delete a VLAN database, you may find that it becomes updated from a server switch because of your VTP mode.

Another serious problem occurs when you take a new switch in server mode (the default mode) and plug it into an existing network. If the VTP revision number is higher on the new switch, it sends an update to all other switches to overwrite their VLAN database with new information—in this case, an empty VLAN data-base. You now have a production network with no VLAN information.

Recommended practice is that you put a switch into VTP client mode before add-ing them into a production network, allow it to receive an update of current VLAN information, and then change it to VTP server mode.

Confirming VTP Configuration

1900 Series Switch

1900Switch#**show vtp**	Displays all VTP information

2900/2950 Series Switch

29x0Switch#**show vtp status**	Displays VTP domain status
29x0Switch#**show vtp counters**	Displays VTP statistics

Inter-VLAN Communication: Router-on-a-Stick

`Router(config)#int fa 0/0`	Enters interface mode for interface fa 0/0
`Router(config-if)#no shut`	Turns the interface on
`Router(config-if)#int fa 0/0.1`	Creates subinterface 0/0.1
`Router(config-subif)#encapsulation dot1q 1 native`	Assigns the native VLAN (usually VLAN 1) to this logical subinterface
`Router(config-subif)#ip address 192.168.1.1 255.255.255.0`	Assigns an IP address to the subinterface
`Router(config-subif)#int fa 0/0.10`	Creates subinterface 0/0.10
`Router(config-subif)#encapsulation dot1q 10`	Assigns VLAN 10 to this subinterface
`Router(config-subif)#ip address 192.168.10.1 255.255.255.0`	Assigns an IP address to the subinterface
`Router(config-subif)#`Ctrl z	
`Router#`	

Router-on-a-Stick Tips

- The 1900 series switch has ISL capability only. If connecting a router to a 1900 series switch, replace the router command **encapsulation dot1q** *x* with **encapsulation isl** *x*.
- The native VLAN (usually VLAN 1) cannot be configured on a logical subinterface in Cisco IOS Software releases earlier than 12.1(3)T. Native IP addresses therefore have to be configured on the physical interface:

```
Router(config)#int fa 0/0
Router(config-if)#encapsulation dot1q 1 native
Router(config-if)#ip address 192.168.1.1 255.255.255.0
Router(config-if)#int fa 0/0.10
Router(config-subif)#encapsulation dot1q 10
Router(config-subif)#ip address 192.168.10.1 255.255.255.0
```

- The 1721 and the 1760 series routers have Dot1Q capability only. They cannot perform ISL encapsulation.
- The 2620 and 2621 series routers have both Dot1Q and ISL encapsulation methods.
- The number of the subinterface can be any number from 0–4294967295.

- Use the same number of the VLAN number for the subinterface number. Troubleshooting VLAN 10 on subinterface fa 0/0.10 is more intuitive than troubleshooting it on fa 0/0.2.

- On a 1721 or 1760 series router, the name of the Fast Ethernet interface is fa 0.x.

- On a 2620 or 2621 series router, the name of the Fast Ethernet interface is fa 0/0.x or 0/1.x.

Configuration Example: VTP and Inter-VLAN Routing

Figure 15-1 shows the network topology for the configuration of VTP and inter-VLAN routing. There are separate sections on configuring both 2900 and 2950 series switches.

Figure 15-1   Network Topology for VTP and Inter-VLAN Routing Configuration

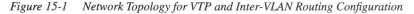

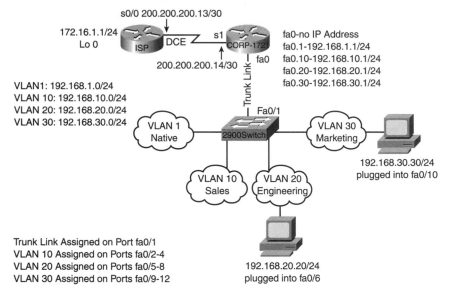

ISP Router

`Router>`**`en`**	
`Router>#`**`config t`**	
`Router(config)#`**`hostname ISP`**	Sets the host name
`ISP(config)#`**`no ip domain-lookup`**	Turns off DNS resolution to avoid wait time due to DNS lookup of spelling errors

`ISP(config)#`**`line con 0`**	
`ISP(config-line)#`**`logging synchronous`**	Appends the command line to a new line—no interruption from info items
`ISP(config-line)#`**`exec-timeout 0 0`**	Console session will never time out
`ISP(config-line)#`**`exit`**	
`ISP(config)#`**`enable secret cisco`**	Sets the secret password to **cisco**
`ISP(config)#`**`int lo 0`**	Creates a loopback address for testing purposes
`ISP(config-if)#`**`description simulated address representing remote website`**	
`ISP(config-if)#`**`ip address 172.16.1.1 255.255.255.0`**	
`ISP(config-if)#`**`int s0/0`**	Enters serial interface configuration mode
`ISP(config-if)#`**`description WAN link to the Corporate Router`**	
`ISP(config-if)#`**`ip address 200.200.200.13 255.255.255.252`**	
`ISP(config-if)#`**`clock 56000`**	Sets the clock rate for the serial link
`ISP(config-if)#`**`no shut`**	
`ISP(config-if)#`**`exit`**	
`ISP(config-if)#`**`router eigrp 10`**	Turns on the EIGRP routing process
`ISP(config-router)#`**`network 172.16.0.0`**	Advertises the 172.16.0.0 network
`ISP(config-router)#`**`network 200.200.200.0`**	Advertises the 200.200.200.0 network
`ISP(config-router)#`**`no auto-summary`**	Turns off automatic summarization at the classful boundary
`ISP(config-router)#`**`exit`**	

`ISP(config)#exit`	
`ISP#copy run start`	Saves the configuration to NVRAM
CORP Router (1721 Router Running Cisco IOS Software Release 12.2(4)	These commands work also for the 1760 and the 2620/2621 series routers
`Router>en`	
`Router#config t`	
`Router(config)#hostname CORP`	Sets host name
`CORP(config)#no ip domain-lookup`	Turns off resolution to avoid wait time due to DNS lookup of spelling errors
`CORP(config)#line con 0`	
`CORP(config-line)#logging synchronous`	Appends the command line to a new line—no interruption from info items
`CORP(config-line)#exec-timeout 0 0`	Console session will never time out
`CORP(config-line)#exit`	
`CORP(config)#enable secret cisco`	Sets the secret password to **cisco**
`CORP(config)#int s1`	
`CORP(config-if)#desc WAN link to ISP Router`	
`CORP(config-if)#ip add 200.200.200.14 255.255.255.252`	
`CORP(config-if)#bandwidth 1544`	Sets bandwidth to 1544 kilobits for EIGRP calculation
`CORP(config-if)#no shut`	
`CORP(config-if)#exit`	
`CORP(config)#int fa0`	

CORP(config-if)#**full duplex**	
CORP(config-if)#**no shut**	
CORP(config-if)#**int fa0.1**	Creates a subinterface
CORP(config-if)#**no ip address**	Ensures there is no IP address assigned to the interface
CORP(config-subif)#**desc Management VLAN 1**	Assigns a description to the subinterface
CORP(config-subif)#**encapsulation dot1q 1 native**	Enables Dot1Q encapsulation with VLAN 1 as the native VLAN
CORP(config-subif)#**ip add 192.168.1.1 255.255.255.0**	Assigns an IP address to the subinterface
CORP(config-subif)#**int fa0.10**	Creates a subinterface
CORP(config-subif)#**desc Sales VLAN 10**	Assigns a description to the subinterface
CORP(config-subif)#**encapsulation dot1q 10**	Enables Dot1Q encapsulation on VLAN 10
CORP(config-subif)#**ip add 192.168.10.1 255.255.255.0**	Assigns an IP address to the subinterface
CORP(config-subif)#**int fa0.20**	Creates a subinterface
CORP(config-subif)#**desc Engineering VLAN 20**	Assigns a description to the subinterface
CORP(config-subif)#**encapsulation dot1q 20**	Enables Dot1Q encapsulation on VLAN 20
CORP(config-subif)#**ip add 192.168.20.1 255.255.255.0**	Assigns an IP address to the subinterface
CORP(config-subif)#**int fa0.30**	Creates a subinterface
CORP(config-subif)#**desc Marketing VLAN 30**	Assigns a description to the subinterface
CORP(config-subif)#**encapsulation dot1q 30**	Enables Dot1Q encapsulation on VLAN 30
CORP(config-subif)#**ip add 192.168.1.1 255.255.255.0**	Assigns an IP address to the subinterface

`CORP(config-subif)#exit`	
`CORP(config)#router eigrp 10`	Turns on the EIGRP routing process
`CORP(config-router)#network 192.168.1.0`	Advertises the 192.168.1.0 network
`CORP(config-router)#network 192.168.10.0`	Advertises the 192.168.10.0 network
`CORP(config-router)#network 192.168.20.0`	Advertises the 192.168.20.0 network
`CORP(config-router)#network 192.168.30.0`	Advertises the 192.168.30.0 network
`CORP(config-router)#network 200.200.200.0`	Advertises the 200.200.200.0 network
`CORP(config-router)#no auto-summary`	Turns off auto summari-zation
`CORP(config-router)#exit`	
`CORP(config)#exit`	
`CORP#copy run start`	Saves the configuration to NVRAM
	Caution: Remember to advertise *all* networks. Advertising 192.168.0.0 does not advertise networks from 192.168.0.0–192.168.255.0. These are separate classful networks, so they must be advertised separately, just like 200.200.200.0 is advertised separately.

2900 Series Switch

`switch>en`	
`switch>#config t`	
`switch(config)#hostname 2900Switch`	Sets host name

`2900Switch(config)#`**`no ip domain-lookup`**	Turns off DNS resolution to avoid wait time due to DNS lookup of spelling errors
`2900Switch(config)#`**`line con 0`**	
`2900Switch(config-line)#`**`logging synchronous`**	Appends the command line to a new line—no interruption from info items
`2900Switch(config-line)#`**`exec-timeout 0 0`**	Console session will never time out
`2900Switch(config-line)#`**`exit`**	
`2900Switch(config)#`**`enable secret cisco`**	Sets the secret password to **cisco**
`2900Switch(config)#`**`exit`**	
`2900Switch#`**`vlan database`**	Enters VLAN database mode
`2900Switch(vlan)#`**`vlan 10 name Sales`**	Creates VLAN 10 with the name Sales
`2900Switch(vlan)#`**`vlan 20 name Engineering`**	Creates VLAN 20 with the name Engineering
`2900Switch(vlan)#`**`vlan 30 name Marketing`**	Creates VLAN 30 with the name Marketing
`2900Switch(vlan)#`**`vtp server`**	Makes the switch a VTP server
`2900Switch(vlan)#`**`vtp domain academy`**	Assigns a domain name of academy
`2900Switch(vlan)#`**`exit`**	Applies all changes to VLAN database and exits mode
`2900Switch#`**`config t`**	
`2900Switch(config)#`**`int vlan1`**	

2900Switch(config-if)#**ip add 192.168.1.2 255.255.255.0**	
2900Switch(config-if)#**no shutdown**	
2900Switch(config-if)#**exit**	
2900Switch(config)#**ip default-gateway 192.168.1.1**	
2900Switch(config)#**int fa 0/1**	
2900Switch(config-if)#**desc Trunk Link to CORP Router**	
2900Switch(config-if)#**switchport mode trunk**	Creates a trunk link
2900Switch(config-if)#**switchport trunk encapsulation dot1q**	Sets encapsulation to Dot1Q
2900Switch(config-if)#**int fa 0/2**	
2900Switch(config-if)#**switchport access vlan 10**	Assigns a port to VLAN 10
2900Switch(config-if)#**spanning-tree portfast**	Transitions the port directly to the Forwarding state in Spanning Tree Protocol (STP)
	Note: The command **switchport mode access** is not needed, because this is the default mode for interfaces. Use it only if the port was previously set to be a trunk link.
2900Switch(config-if)#**int fa0/3**	
2900Switch(config-if)#**switchport access vlan 10**	Assigns a port to VLAN 10
2900Switch(config-if)#**spanning-tree portfast**	Transitions the port directly to the Forwarding state in STP
2900Switch(config-if)#**int fa0/4**	
2900Switch(config-if)#**switchport access vlan 10**	Assigns a port to VLAN 10

`2900Switch(config-if)#`**`spanning-tree portfast`**	Transitions the port directly to the Forwarding state in STP
`2900Switch(config-if)#`**`int fa0/5`**	
`2900Switch(config-if)#`**`switchport access vlan 20`**	Assigns a port to VLAN 20
`2900Switch(config-if)#`**`spanning-tree portfast`**	Transitions the port directly to the Forwarding state in STP
`2900Switch(config-if)#`**`int fa0/6`**	
`2900Switch(config-if)#`**`switchport access vlan 20`**	Assigns a port to VLAN 20
`2900Switch(config-if)#`**`spanning-tree portfast`**	Transitions the port directly to the Forwarding state in STP
`2900Switch(config-if)#`**`int fa0/7`**	
`2900Switch(config-if)#`**`switchport access vlan 20`**	Assigns a port to VLAN 20
`2900Switch(config-if)#`**`spanning-tree portfast`**	Transitions the port directly to the Forwarding state in STP
`2900Switch(config-if)#`**`int fa0/8`**	
`2900Switch(config-if)#`**`switchport access vlan 20`**	Assigns a port to VLAN 20
`2900Switch(config-if)#`**`spanning-tree portfast`**	Transitions the port directly to the Forwarding state in STP
`2900Switch(config-if)#`**`int fa0/9`**	
`2900Switch(config-if)#`**`switchport access vlan 30`**	Assigns a port to VLAN 30
`2900Switch(config-if)#`**`spanning-tree portfast`**	Transitions the port directly to the Forwarding state in STP
`2900Switch(config-if)#`**`int fa0/10`**	

`2900Switch(config-if)#`**`switchport access vlan 30`**	Assigns a port to VLAN 30
`2900Switch(config-if)#`**`spanning-tree portfast`**	Transitions the port directly to the Forwarding state in STP
`2900Switch(config-if)#`**`int fa0/11`**	
`2900Switch(config-if)#`**`switchport access vlan 30`**	Assigns a port to VLAN 30
`2900Switch(config-if)#`**`spanning-tree portfast`**	Transitions the port directly to the Forwarding state in STP
`2900Switch(config-if)#`**`int fa0/12`**	
`2900Switch(config-if)#`**`switchport access vlan 30`**	Assigns a port to VLAN 30
`2900Switch(config-if)#`**`spanning-tree portfast`**	Transitions the port directly to the Forwarding state in STP
`2900Switch(config-if)#`**Ctrl Z**	
`2900Switch#`**`copy run start`**	Saves the configuration to NVRAM
`2900Switch#`	

2950 Series Switch

`switch>`**`en`**	
`switch>#`**`config t`**	
`switch(config)#`**`hostname 2950Switch`**	Sets the host name
`2950Switch(config)#`**`no ip domain-lookup`**	Turns off DNS resolution to avoid wait time due to DNS lookup of spelling errors
`2950Switch(config)#`**`line con 0`**	
`2950Switch(config-line)#`**`logging synchronous`**	Appends the command line to a new line—no interruption from info items

`2950Switch(config-line)#`**`exec-timeout 0 0`**	Console session will never time out
`2950Switch(config-line)#`**`exit`**	
`2950Switch(config)#`**`enable secret cisco`**	Sets the secret password to **cisco**
`2950Switch(config)#`**`vlan 10`**	Creates VLAN 10
`2950Switch(config-vlan)#`**`name Sales`**	Defines the name of Sales
`2950Switch(config-vlan)#`**`vlan 20`**	Creates VLAN 20
`2950Switch(config-vlan)#`**`name Engineering`**	Defines the name of Engineering
`2950Switch(config-vlan)#`**`vlan 30`**	Creates VLAN 30
`2950Switch(config-vlan)#`**`name Marketing`**	Defines the name of Marketing
`2950Switch(config-vlan)#`**`exit`**	
`2950Switch(config)#`**`vtp mode server`**	Makes the switch a VTP server
`2950Switch(config)#`**`vtp domain academy`**	Assigns a domain name of academy
`2950Switch(config)#`**`int vlan1`**	Creates the virtual VLAN 1 interface
`2950Switch(config-if)#`**`ip add 192.168.1.2`** **`255.255.255.0`**	Assigns an IP address to the interface
`2950Switch(config-if)#`**`no shutdown`**	
`2950Switch(config-if)#`**`exit`**	
`2950Switch(config)#`**`ip default-gateway`** **`192.168.1.1`**	Assigns the IP address of the default gateway
`2950Switch(config)#`**`int fa 0/1`**	
`2950Switch(config-if)#`**`desc Trunk Link to CORP`** **`Router`**	
`2950Switch(config-if)#`**`switchport mode trunk`**	Creates a trunk link
`2950Switch(config-if)#`**`int range fa 0/2 - 4`**	

`2950Switch(config-if-range)#`**`switchport access vlan 10`**	Assigns ports to VLAN 10
`2950Switch(config-if-range)#`**`spanning-tree portfast`**	Transitions ports directly to the Forwarding state in STP
	Note: The command **switchport mode access** is not needed, because this is the default mode for interfaces. Use it only if the port was previously set to be a trunk link.
`2950Switch(config-if-range)#`**`int range fa0/5 - 8`**	
`2950Switch(config-if-range)#`**`switchport access vlan 20`**	Assigns ports to VLAN 20
`2950Switch(config-if-range)#`**`spanning-tree portfast`**	Transitions ports directly to the Forwarding state in STP
`2950Switch(config-if-range)#`**`int range fa0/9 - 12`**	
`2950Switch(config-if-range)#`**`switchport access vlan 30`**	Assigns ports to VLAN 10
`2950Switch(config-if-range)#`**`spanning-tree portfast`**	Transitions ports directly to the Forwarding state in STP
`2950Switch(config-if-range)#`**`Ctrl z`**	
`2950Switch#`**`copy run start`**	Saves the configuration to NVRAM

PART VI

Network Administration and Troubleshooting

Chapter 16 Backing Up and Restoring Cisco IOS Software
and Configurations

Chapter 17 Password Recovery Procedures and the
Configuration Register

Chapter 18 CDP

Chapter 19 Telnet

Chapter 20 Ping and Traceroute

Chapter 21 SNMP and Syslog

Chapter 22 Basic Troubleshooting

Backing Up and Restoring Cisco IOS Software and Configurations

This chapter provides information and commands concerning the following topics:

- Changing the order of from where IOS is loaded
- Pre-IOS 12.0 commands versus 12.x commands
- Backing up and restoring configurations and IOS using TFTP
- Restoring IOS using Xmodem
- Restoring IOS using **tftpdnld**
- Upgrading firmware
- Copying IOS to a TFTP Server

Boot System Commands

`Router(config)#boot system flash` *image-name*	Loads IOS with *image-name*
`Router(config)#boot system tftp` *image-name* `172.16.10.3`	Loads IOS with *image-name* from a TFTP server
`Router(config)#boot system rom`	Loads IOS from ROM
`Router(config)#exit`	
`Router#copy run start`	Saves running-configuration to NVRAM. Router will execute commands in order they were entered on next reload

If you enter **boot system flash** first, that is the first place the router will go to look for the IOS. If you want to go to a TFTP server first, make sure that the **boot system tftp** command is the first one you enter.

Cisco IOS Software Prerelease 12.0 Commands Versus Cisco IOS Software 12.x Commands

Pre-IOS 12.0 Commands	IOS 12.x Commands
copy tftp running-config	**copy tftp: system:running-config**
copy tftp startup-config	**copy tftp: nvram:startup-config**
show startup-config	**more nvram:startup-config**
erase startup-config	**erase nvram:**
copy run start	**copy system:running-config nvram:startup-config**
copy run tftp	**copy system:running-config tftp:**
show run	**more system:running-config**

Backing Up Configurations

Denver#**copy run start**	Saves running-config from DRAM to NVRAM (locally)
Denver#**copy run tftp**	Copies running-config to remote TFTP server
Address or name of remote host[ ]? **192.168.119.20**	IP address of TFTP server
Destination Filename [Denver-confg]?⏎Enter	Name to use for file saved on TFTP server
!!!!!!!!!!!!!!!!	Each bang symbol (!) = 1 datagram of data
624 bytes copied in 7.05 secs	
Denver#	File has been transferred successfully

NOTE: You can also use the preceding sequence for a **copy start tftp** command sequence.

Restoring Configurations

Denver#`copy tftp run`	Copies configuration file from TFTP server to DRAM
Address or name of remote host[ ]? 192.168.119.20	IP address of TFTP server
Source filename [ ]?**Denver-confg**	Enter the name of the file you want to retrieve
Destination filename [running-config]?⊣Enter	
Accessing tftp://192.168.119.20/Denver-confg…	
Loading Denver-confg from 192.168.119.02 (via Fast Ethernet 0/0):	
!!!!!!!!!!!!!!	
[OK-624 bytes]	
624 bytes copied in 9.45 secs	
Denver#	File has been transferred successfully

NOTE: You can also use the preceding sequence for a **copy tftp start** command sequence.

Backing Up IOS to a TFTP Server

Denver#`copy flash tftp`	
Source filename [ ]? **c2600-js-l_121-3.bin**	Name of IOS image
Address or name of remote host [ ]? **192.168.119.20**	Address of TFTP server
Destination filename [c2600-js-l_121-3.bin]?⊣Enter	Destination filename is the same as the source filename, so just press ⊣Enter

!!! !!!	
8906589 bytes copied in 263.68 seconds	
Denver#	

Restoring/Upgrading IOS from a TFTP Server

Denver#**copy tftp flash**	
Address or name of remote host [ ]? **192.168.119.20**	
Source filename [ ]? **c2600-js-l_121-3.bin**	
Destination filename [c2600-js-l_121- 3.bin]?⏎Enter	
Accessing tftp://192.168.119.20/c2600-js- l_121-3.bin	
Erase flash: before copying? [confirm]⏎Enter	If Flash memory is full, must erase it first
Erasing the flash file system will remove all files	
Continue? [confirm]⏎Enter	Press Ctrl c if you want to cancel
Erasing device eeeeeeeeeeeeeeeeee...erased	Each e represents data being erased
Loading c2600-js-l_121-3.bin from 192.168.119.20	
(via) FastEthernet 0/0): !! !! !!!	Each bang symbol (!) = 1 datagram of data
Verifying Check sum .... OK	
[OK – 8906589 Bytes]	
8906589 bytes copied in 277.45 secs	
Denver#	Success

Restoring IOS from ROMmon Mode Using Xmodem

The output that follows was taken from a 1720 router. Some of this output might vary from yours, depending on the router model that you are using.

`rommon 1 >`**`confreg`**	Shows configuration summary. Step through the questions, answering defaults until you can change the console baud rate. Change it to **115200**; makes transfer go faster
| ```
        Configuration Summary
enabled are:
load rom after netboot fails
console baud: 9600
boot: image specified by the boot
system commands
        or default to: cisco2-c1700
``` | |
| ```
do you wish to change the
configuration? y/n [n]: y
enable    "diagnostic mode"? y/n [n]: n
enable    "use net in IP bcast address"?
y/n [n]: n
disable   "load rom after netboot
fails"? y/n [n]: n
enable    "use all zero broadcast"? y/n
[n]: n
enable    "break/abort has effect"? y/n
[n]: n
enable    "ignore system config info"?
y/n [n]: n
change console baud rate? y/n [n]: y
enter rate: 0=9600, 1=4800, 2=1200,
3=2400
                4=19200, 5=38400,
6=57600, 7=115200 [0]: 7
change the boot characteristics? y/n
[n]: n
``` | Prompts will begin to ask a series of questions that will allow you to change the config-register. Answer **n** to all questions except the one that asks you to change the console baud rate. For the enter rate, choose **7** because that is the number that represents a baud rate of 115200 |

``` Configuration Summary enabled are: load rom after netboot fails console baud: 115200 boot: image specified by the boot system commands or default to: cisco2-c1700 do you wish to change the configuration? y/n [n]: n rommon2> ```	After the summary is shown again, choose **n** to not change the configuration and go to the **rommon>** prompt again
`rommon 2>`**reset**	Reloads router at new com speed. Change HyperTerminal setting to **115200** to match the router's new console setting
`Rommon 1>`**xmodem c1700-js-l_121-3.bin**	Asking to transfer this image using Xmodem
`…<output cut>…`	
`Do you wish to continue? y/n [n ]:`**y**	Choose **y** to continue
	In HyperTerminal, go to Transfer, then Send File (see Figure 16-1). Locate the IOS file on the hard drive and click Send (see Figure 16-2)
`Router will reload when transfer is completed`	
`Reset baud rate on router`	

Router(config)#**line con 0**	
Router(config-line)#**speed 9600**	
Router(config-line)#**exit**	HyperTerminal will stop responding. Reconnect to the router using 9600 baud, 8-N-1

Figure 16-1   Finding the IOS Image File

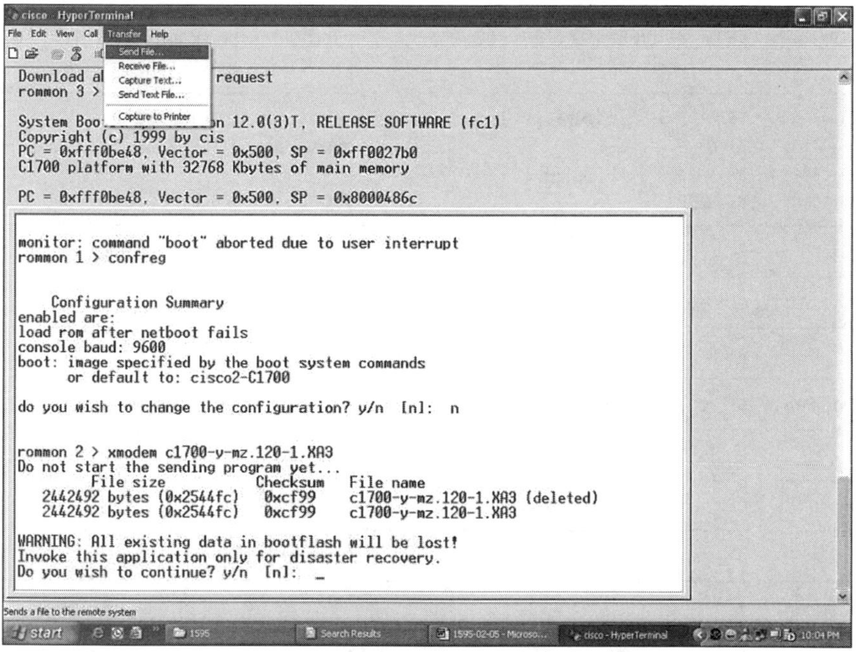

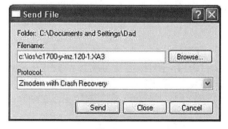

Figure 16-2   Sending the IOS Image File to the Router

Restoring the IOS Using the ROMmon Environmental Variables and tftpdnld Command

`rommon 1>IP_ADDRESS=192.168.100.1`	Indicates the IP address for this unit
`rommon 2>IP_SUBNET_MASK=255.255.255.0`	Indicates the subnet mask for this unit
`rommon 3>DEFAULT_GATEWAY=192.168.100.1`	Indicates the default gateway for this unit
`rommon 4>TFTP_SERVER=192.168.100.2`	Indicates the IP address of the TFTP server
`rommon 5>TFTP_FILE= c2600-js-l_121-3.bin`	Indicates the filename to fetch from the TFTP server
`rommon 6>tftpdnld`	Starts the process
`…<output cut>…`	
`Do you wish to continue? y/n:  [n]:y`	
`…<output cut>…`	
`Rommon 7>i`	Resets the router. **i** stands for initialize

NOTE: Commands and environmental variables are case sensitive, so be sure that you have not accidentally added spaces between variables and answers.

Upgrading Catalyst 1900 Firmware with a TFTP Server

To upgrade the Catalyst 1900 series switch firmware with a TFTP server, you must use the interactive menu.

Select option **F** from main menu	F for firmware
Select option **S** from Firmware menu	S for TFTP server

Enter in address for TFTP server	
Select option **F** from Firmware menu	F for firmware upgrade filename
Enter name of firmware upgrade file	
Select option **T** from Firmware menu	Initiates TFTP upgrade
Switch will reset itself automatically and load new firmware	

Copying IOS to TFTP Server

2900 Series Switch

2900Switch#`copy flash:c2900XL-hs-mz-112.8.10-SA6.bin tftp`	Same procedure as with router
`Source filename [c2900XL-hs-mz-112.8.10-SA6.bin]?`	Just press `↵Enter`
`Destination IP address or hostname [ ]` **192.168.1.3**	Address of TFTP server
`Destination filename [c2900XL-hs-mz-112.8.10-SA6.bin]?`	Just press `↵Enter`
`!!!!!!!!!!!!!!!!!!!!!!!!!!!!!!!!!!!!!!!!!!!!!!!` `!!!!!!!!!!!!!!!!!!!!!!!!!!!!!!!!!!!!!!!!!!!!!!!` `!!!!!!!!!!!!!!!!!!!!!!!!!!!!!!!!!!!!!!!!!!!!!!!` `!!!!!!!!!!!!!!!!!!!!!`	Each bang symbol (!) = 1 datagram sent
`<output cut>`	
`1119104 bytes copied in 21.43 secs`	
2900Switch#	

2950 Series Switch

2950Switch#`copy flash tftp`	Same procedure as with router

Source filename [ ]? **c2950-c3h2s-mz.120-5.3.WC.1.bin**	
Destination IP address or hostname [ ] **192.168.1.3**	Address of TFTP server
Destination filename [c2950-c3h2s-mz.120-5.3.WC.1.bin]?	Just press Ｅｎｔｅｒ
!!! !!! !!! !!!!!!!!!!!!!!!!!!!!!	Each bang symbol (!) = 1 datagram sent
<output cut>	
1674921 bytes copied in 31.542 secs	
2950Switch#	

Firmware Upgrade of Catalyst 2950 Series Switches

2950Switch#**archive tar /x tftp:// 192.168.1.3/c2950-c3h2s-mz.120-5.3.WC.1.tar flash:**	Extracts a new IOS image into Flash memory. The image c2950-c3h2s-mz.120-5.3.WC.1.tar must be on the TFTP server located at 192.168.1.3
2950Switch(config)#**boot system flash c2950-c3h2s-mz.120-5.3.WC.1.bin**	Switch will now boot to this IOS
2950Switch(config)#**exit**	
2950Switch#**reload**	Restarts the switch

NOTE: Tape Archive (TAR) is a compression format used in the transfer of files. TAR is a UNIX utility.

BIN is an abbreviation for the word *binary*. A binary (.bin) file is a file containing information in binary form.

Because Cisco IOS Software was based originally on a UNIX platform, IOS images are *.bin* or *.tar* files.

Configuration Example: 2900 Series Switch

Figure 16-3 shows the network topology for the basic configuration of a 2900 series switch using the commands covered in this chapter.

Figure 16-3   Network Topology for 2900 Series Switch Configuration

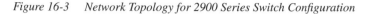
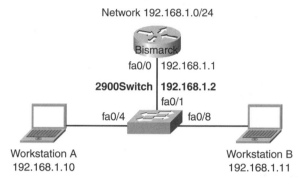

Network 192.168.1.0/24

Bismarck

fa0/0 | 192.168.1.1

2900Switch | **192.168.1.2**

fa0/1

fa0/4   fa0/8

Workstation A   Workstation B
192.168.1.10   192.168.1.11

`switch>`**`en`**	Enters privileged mode
`switch#`**`config t`**	Enters global config mode
`switch(config)#`**`no ip domain-lookup`**	Turns off DNS queries so that spelling mistakes will not slow you down
`switch(config)#`**`hostname 2900`**	Sets host name
`2900(config)#`**`enable secret cisco`**	Sets encrypted secret password to **cisco**
`2900(config)#`**`line con 0`**	Enters line console mode
`2900(config-line)#`**`logging synchronous`**	Appends commands to new line; router information will not interrupt
`2900(config-line)#`**`login`**	User must log in to console before use
`2900(config-line)#`**`password switch`**	Sets password to **switch**
`2900(config-line)#`**`exec-timeout 0 0`**	Console will never log out
`2900(config-line)#`**`exit`**	Moves back to global config mode

`2900(config)#line aux 0`	Moves to line auxiliary mode
`2900(config-line)#login`	User must log in to auxiliary port before use
`2900(config-line)#password class`	Sets password to **class**
`2900(config-line)#exit`	Back to global config mode
`2900(config)#line vty 0 15`	Moves to configure all 16 vty ports at same time
`2900(config-line)#login`	User must log in to vty port before use
`2900(config-line)#password class`	Sets password to **class**
`2900(config-line)#exit`	Back to global config mode
`2900(config)#ip default-gateway 192.168.1.1`	Sets default gateway
`2900(config)#int vlan 1`	Moves to virtual interface VLAN 1
`2900(config-if)#ip add 192.168.1.2 255.255.255.0`	Sets IP address for switch
`2900(config-if)#no shut`	Turns virtual interface on
`2900(config-if)#int fa 0/1`	Moves to interface fa 0/1
`2900(config-if)#desc Link to Router`	Sets local description
`2900(config-if)#int fa 0/4`	Moves to interface fa 0/4
`2900(config-if)#desc Link to Workstation A`	Sets local description
`2900(config-if)#port security`	Activates port security
`2900(config-if)#port security max-mac-count 1`	Only one MAC address will be allowed in the MAC table
`2900(config-if)#port security action shutdown`	Port will be turned off if more than one MAC address is reported
`2900(config-if)#int fa 0/8`	Moves to interface fa 0/8
`2900(config-if)#desc Link to Workstation B`	Sets local description

`2900(config-if)#`**`port security`**	Activates port security
`2900(config-if)#`**`port security max-mac-count 1`**	Only one MAC address will be allowed in the MAC table
`2900(config-if)#`**`port security action shutdown`**	Port will be turned off if more than one MAC address is reported
`2900(config-if)#`**`exit`**	Returns to global config mode
`2900(config)#`**`exit`**	Returns to privileged mode
`2900#`**`copy run start`**	Saved configuration to NVRAM
`2900#`	

CHAPTER 17

Password Recovery Procedures and the Configuration Register

This chapter provides information and commands concerning the following topics:

- The configuration register
  - How to verify it
  - How to change it
  - What it looks like
  - What the bits mean
  - The boot field
  - Console Terminal Baud Rate Settings
  - Changing the console line speed—CLI
  - Changing the console line speed—ROM Monitor Mode
- Password recovery procedures for Cisco routers
- Password recovery procedures for 1900 Series Catalyst Switches
- Password recovery procedures for 2900/2950 Series Catalyst Switches

The Configuration Register

router#**show version**	Last line of output tells you what the configuration register is set to
router#**config t**	
router(config)#**config-register 0x2142**	Changes the configuration register to 2142

The Configuration Register: A Visual Representation

The configuration register is a 16-bit field stored in NVRAM. The bits are numbered from 15 to 0 looking at the bit stream from left to right. Bits are split up into groups of 4, and each group is represented by a hexadecimal digit.

15 14 13 12	11 10 9 8	7 6 5 4	3 2 1 0	Bit places
0 0 1 0	0 0 0 1	0 1 0 0	0 0 1 0	Register bits
2	1	4	2	Bits represented in hex

The Configuration Register—What the Bits Mean

Bit Number	Hexadecimal	Meaning
00–03	0x0000 – 0x000F	Boot Field
06	0x0040	Ignore NVRAM contents
07	0x0080	OEM bit enabled
08	0x0100	Break disabled
09	0x0200	Cause system to use secondary bootstrap (typically not used)
10	0x0400	IP broadcast with all zeros
5, 11, 12	0x0020, 0x0800, 0x1000	Console line speed
13	0x2000	Boots default ROM software if network boot fails
14	0x4000	IP broadcasts do not have net numbers
15	0x8000	Enables diagnostic messages and ignores NVRAM contents

The Boot Field

NOTE: Even though there are 16 possible combinations in the boot field, there are only three that are used.

Boot Field	Meaning
00	Stays at the ROM Monitor on a reload or power cycle
01	Boots the first image in Flash memory as a system image
02 – F	Enables default booting from Flash memory Enables **boot system** commands that override default booting from Flash memory

TIP: Because the default boot field has 14 different ways to represent it, a configuration register setting of 0x2102 is the same as 0x2109, or 210F. The **boot system** command is described in Chapter 16, "Backing Up and Restoring Cisco IOS Software and Configuration."

Console Terminal Baud Rate Settings

Baud	Bit 5	Bit 12	Bit 11
115200	1	1	1
57600	1	1	0
38400	1	0	1
19200	1	0	0
9600	0	0	0
4800	0	0	1
2400	0	1	1
1200	0	1	0

Changing the Console Line Speed—CLI

`router#config t`	
`router(config)#line console 0`	Enters console line mode
`router(config-line)#speed 19200`	Changes speed to 19200 baud

TIP: Cisco IOS software does not allow you to change the console speed bits directly with the **config-register** command.

Changing the Console Line Speed—ROM Monitor Mode—1700/2600 Series

`rommon1>confreg`	Shows configuration summary. Step through the questions, answering with the defaults until you can change the console baud rate

`  Configuration Summary`
`enabled are:`
`load rom after netboot fails`
`console baud:  9600`
`boot:  image specified by the boot system commands`
`    or default to: x (name of system image)`	

do you wish to change the configuration? y/n [n]: **y** enable "diagonstic mode"? y/n [n]: **n** enable "use net in IP bcast address"? y/n [n]: **n** disable "load rom after netboot fails"? y/n [n]: **n** enable "use all zero broadcast"? y/n [n]: **n** enable "break/abort has effect"? y/n [n]: **n** enable "ignore system config info"? y/n [n]: **n** change console baud rate? y/n [n]: **y** enter rate: 0=9600, 1=4800, 2=1200, 3=2400 4=19200, 5=38400, 6=57600, 7=115200 [0]: **7**	
Configuration Summary enabled are: load rom after netboot fails console baud: 115200 boot: image specified by the boot system commands or default to: *x* (name of system image)	
change the boot characteristics? y/n [n]: **n**	After the summary is shown again, choose **n** to not change the configuration and go to the rommon> prompt again
rommon2>	

TIP: Make sure that after you change the console baud rate, you change your terminal program to match the same rate!

Password Recovery Procedures for Cisco Routers

Step	2500 Series Commands	1700/2600 Series Commands
Step 1: Boot the router and interrupt the boot sequence as soon as text appears on the screen.	Press Ctrl Break >	Press Ctrl Break rommon 1>

Step 2: Change the configuration register to ignore contents of NVRAM.	`>o/r 0x2142`	`rommon 1>`**`confreg 0x2142`**
	`>`	`rommon 2>`
Step 3: Reload the router.	`>i`	`rommon 2>`**`reset`**
Step 4: Enter privileged mode. (Do not enter setup mode.)	`Router>`**`en`**	`Router>`**`en`**
	`Router#`	`Router#`
Step 5: Copy startup-config into running-config.	`Router#`**`copy start run`**	`Router#`**`copy start run`**
	`…<output cut>…`	`…<output cut>…`
	`Denver#`	`Denver#`
Step 6: Change the password.	`Denver#`**`config t`**	`Denver#`**`config t`**
	`Denver(config)#`**`enable secret`** *`new`*	`Denver(config)#`**`enable secret`** *`new`*
	`Denver(config)#`	`Denver(config)#`
Step 7: Reset configuration register back to default value.	`Denver(config)#`**`config-register 0x2102`**	`Denver(config)#`**`config-register 0x2102`**
	`Denver(config)#`	`Denver(config)#`
Step 8: Save the configuration.	`Denver(config)#`**`exit`**	`Denver(config)#`**`exit`**
	`Denver#`**`copy run start`**	`Denver#`**`copy run start`**
	`Denver#`	`Denver#`

Step 9: Verify configuration register.	Denver#**show version**	Denver#**show version**
	...\<output cut>...	...\<output cut>...
	Configuration register is 0x2142 (will be 0x2102 at next reload)	Configuration register is 0x2142 (will be 0x2102 at next reload)
	Denver#	Denver#
Step 10: Reload the router.	Denver#**reload**	Denver#**reload**

Password Recovery for 1900 Series Switches

Unplug the power supply from the back of the switch	
Press and hold the Mode button on the front of the switch	
Plug the switch back in	
Wait until the LED above port 1X goes out, and then release the Mode button	This allows you to access the Systems-Engineering menu, which is a diagnostic menu for troubleshooting issues
Press ⏎**Enter** to continue	
Press ⏎**Enter** to display the Systems-Engineering menu	Note which firmware version is on the switch

Password Recovery for
Firmware 1.10 or Later

Power-cycle the switch	Unplug, then plug the switch back in
After POST complete, you see the following:	

Do you wish to clear the passwords? [**Y**]es or [**N**]o	You have 10 seconds to respond
Enter **Y** to delete the password	
Assign a new password from either the menu console or the CLI	As per the section on assigning passwords in this chapter

	Valid on Firmware Between
To View the Password You Are Trying to Recover	**1.10 and 3.02**
Unplug the power supply from the back of the switch	
Press and hold the Mode button on the front of the switch	
Plug the switch back in	
Wait until the LED above port 1X goes out, then release the Mode button	This allows you to access the Systems-Engineering menu, which is a diagnostic menu for troubleshooting issues
Press ⏎**Enter** to continue	
Press ⏎**Enter**	
Select **S** on the Diagnostic-Console Systems= Engineering menu	
Select **V** on the System-Debug interface	Displays the management console password
Select **M** option on the Console Settings menu	

**Password Recovery for Firmware 1.09
and Earlier**

You must contact Cisco Technical Assistance Center (TAC)	
Make sure you have the switch serial number or MAC address of the switch	

Password Recovery for 2900/2950 Series Switches

Unplug the power supply from the back of the switch	
Press and hold the Mode button on the front of the switch	
Plug the switch back in	
Wait until the LED above port 1X goes out, then release the Mode button	For the 2900 series switch
or	
Wait until the STAT LED goes out, then release the Mode button	For the 2950 series switch
Issue the following commands:	
switch: `flash_init`	Initializes the Flash memory
switch: `load_helper`	
switch: `flash:`	Do not forget the colon. This displays what files are in Flash memory
switch: `rename flash:config.text flash:config.old`	The config.text file contains the password
switch: `boot`	Boots the switch
Type **n** to exit the initial configuration dialog	Takes you to user mode
switch>**en**	Enters privileged mode
switch#**rename flash:config.old flash:config.text**	Renames the file back to the original name
Destination filename [config.text]	Press ↵Enter

switch#**copy flash:config.text** **system:running-config**	Copies config file into memory
768 bytes copied in 0.624 seconds	
2900Switch#	Config file is now reloaded
2900Switch#**config t**	Enters global configuration mode
2900Switch(config)#	
Proceed to change the passwords as needed	
2900Switch(config)#**exit**	
2900Switch#**copy run start**	Saves config with new passwords

CHAPTER 18

CDP

This chapter provides information and commands concerning the following topic:

- Cisco Discovery Protocol (CDP)

Cisco Discovery Protocol

`Router#`**`show cdp`**	Displays global CDP information (such as timers)
`Router#`**`show cdp neighbors`**	Displays information about neighbors
`Router#`**`show cdp neighbors detail`**	Displays more detail about neighbor device
`Router#`**`show cdp entry word`**	Displays information about device named word
`Router#`**`show cdp entry *`**	Displays information about all devices
`Router#`**`show cdp interface`**	Displays info about interfaces that have CDP running
`Router#`**`show cdp interface x`**	Displays info about specific interface x running CDP
`Router#`**`show cdp traffic`**	Displays traffic info—packets in/out/version
`Router(config)#`**`cdp holdtime x`**	Changes length of time to keep CDP packets
`Router(config)#`**`cdp timer x`**	Changes how often CDP updates are sent
`Router(config)#`**`cdp run`**	Enables CDP globally (on by default)
`Router(config)#`**`no cdp run`**	Turns off CDP globally
`Router(config-if)#`**`cdp enable`**	Enables CDP on a specific interface

`Router(config-if)#no cdp enable`	Turns off CDP on a specific interface
`Router#clear cdp counters`	Resets traffic counters to 0
`Router#clear cdp table`	Deletes the CDP table
`Router#debug cdp adjacency`	Monitors CDP neighbor information
`Router#debug cdp events`	Monitors all CDP events
`Router#debug cdp ip`	Monitors CDP events specifically for IP
`Router#debug cdp packets`	Monitors CDP packet-related information

CAUTION: Although CDP is an excellent source of information to you the network administrator, is it a potential security risk if a hacker gains access to one of your systems. The information that you gain through CDP is also gained by the hacker.

After you have used CDP to gather your information in a production environment, turn it off to thwart any bad people from using it for no good.

CHAPTER 19

Telnet

This chapter provides information and commands concerning the following topics:

- Using Telnet to remotely connect to other devices

Telnet

The following five commands all achieve the same result—the attempt to connect remotely to the router named paris at IP address 172.16.20.1.

Denver>**telnet paris**	Enter if **ip host** command was used previously to create a mapping of an IP address to the word paris
Denver>**telnet 172.16.20.1**	
Denver>**paris**	Enter if **ip host** command is using default port #
Denver>**connect paris**	
Denver>**172.16.20.1**	

Any of the preceding commands lead to the following configuration sequence:

Paris>	As long as vty password is set. See Caution following this table
Paris>**exit**	Terminates the Telnet session
Denver>	
Paris>**logout**	Terminates the Telnet session
Denver>	
Paris>Ctrl ⬆Shift 6, release, then press x	Suspends the Telnet session, but does not terminate it
Denver>	

`Denver>`⏎Enter	Resumes the connection to paris
`Paris>`	
`Denver>`**resume**	Resumes the connection to paris
`Paris>`	
`Denver>`**disconnect paris**	Terminates the session to paris
`Denver>`	
`Denver#`**show sessions**	Displays connections you opened to other sites
`Denver#`**show users**	Displays who is connected remotely to you
`Denver#`**clear line** *x*	Disconnects remote user connected to you on line *x* Line number is listed in the output gained from the **show users** command
`Denver(config)#`**line vty 0 4**	
`Denver(config-line)` **session-limit** *x*	Limits the number of simultaneous sessions per vty line to *x* amount

CAUTION: The following configuration creates a big security hole. Never use it in a live production environment. Use it in the lab only!

`Denver(config)#`**line vty 0 4**	.
`Denver(config-line)#`**no password**	Remote user is not challenged when Telnetting to this device
`Denver(config-line)#`**no login**	Remote user moves straight to user mode

NOTE: A device must have two passwords for a remote user to be able to make changes to your configuration:

• Line vty password (or have it explicitly turned off; see previous Caution)

• Enable or enable secret password

Without the enable or enable secret password, a remote user will only be able to get to user mode, not to privileged mode. This is extra security.

ping and traceroute

This chapter provides information and commands concerning the following topics:

- ICMP redirect messages
- The **ping** command
- The **traceroute** command

ICMP Redirect Messages

`Router(config-if)#no ip redirects`	Disables ICMP redirects from this specific interface
`Router(config-if)#ip redirects`	Re-enables ICMP redirects from this specific interface

ping Command

`Router#ping w.x.y.z`	Checks for Layer 3 connectivity with device at address *w.x.y.z*
`Router#ping`	Enters extended ping mode, which provides more options

The following table describes the possible **ping** output characters.

Character	Meaning
!	Successful receipt of a reply
.	Device timed out while waiting for reply
U	A destination unreachable error PDU was received
Q	Source quench (destination too busy)
M	Could not fragment
?	Unknown packet type
&	Packet lifetime exceeded

ping

`Router#ping 172.168.20.1`	Performs basic Layer 3 test to address
`Router#ping paris`	Same as above but through IP host name
`Router#ping`	Enters extended ping mode. Can now change parameters of ping test
`Protocol [ip]:` ↵Enter	Press ↵Enter to use ping for IP
`Target IP address: 172.16.20.1`	Enter target IP address
`Repeat count [5]:100`	Enter number of echo requests you want to send. 5 is the default
`Datagram size [100]:`↵Enter	Enter size of datagrams being sent. 100 is the default
`Timeout in Seconds [2]:`↵Enter	Enter timeout delay between sending echo requests
`Extended commands [n]: yes`	Allows you to configure extended commands
`Source address or interface: 10.0.10.1`	Allows you to explicitly set where the pings are originating from
`Type of Service [0]`	Allows you to set the TOS field in the IP Header
`Set DF bit in IP header [no]`	Allows you to set the DF bit in the IP Header
`Validate reply data? [no]`	Allows you to set whether you want validation

Data Pattern [0xABCD]	Allows you to change the data pattern in the data field of the ICMP Echo request packet
Loose, Strict, Record, Timestamp, Verbose[none]: ⏎Enter Sweep range of sizes [no]: ⏎Enter Type escape sequence to abort Sending 100, 100-byte ICMP Echos to 172.16.20.1, timeout is 2 seconds: !! !! !!!!!!!!!!!!!!!!!!!!!!!!!!!!!!!!!!!!! Success rate is 100 percent (100/100) round-trip min/avg/max = 1/1/4 ms	

traceroute

Router#**traceroute 172.168.20.1**	Discovers route taken to travel to destination
Router#**trace paris**	Short form of command with IP host name

CHAPTER 21

SNMP and Syslog

This chapter provides information and commands concerning the following topics:

- Configuring Simple Network Management Protocol (SNMP)
- Configuring Syslog

Configuring SNMP

`Router(config)#snmp-server community academy ro`	Sets a read-only (**ro**) community string called **academy**
`Router(config)#snmp-server community academy rw`	Sets a read-write (**rw**) community string called **academy**
`Router(config)#snmp-server location 2nd Floor IDF`	Defines an SNMP string that describes the physical location of the SNMP server
`Router(config)#snmp-server contact Scott Empson 555-5236`	Defines an SNMP string that describes the sysContact information

NOTE: A community string is like a password. In the case of the first command, the community string grants you access to SNMP.

Configuring Syslog

`Router(config)#logging on`	Enables logging to all supported destinations
`Router(config)#logging 192.168.10.53`	Logging messages will be sent to a syslog server host at address 192.168.10.53
`Router(config)#logging sysadmin`	Logging messages will be sent to a syslog server host named sysadmin

Router(config)#**logging trap x**	Sets the syslog server logging level to value *x*, where *x* is a number between 0 and 7 or a word defining the level. The table that follows provides more details
Router(config)#**service timestamps log datetime**	Syslog messages will now have a timestamp included

There are eight levels of severity in logging messages, as follows:

0	Emergencies	System is unusable
1	Alerts	Immediate action needed
2	Critical	Critical conditions
3	Errors	Error conditions
4	Warnings	Warning conditions
5	Notifications	Normal but significant conditions
6	Informational	Informational messages (default level)
7	Debugging	Debugging messages

Setting a level means you will get that level and everything below it. Level 6 means you will receive level 6 and 7 messages. Level 4 means you will get levels 4 through 7.

Basic Troubleshooting

This chapter provides information and commands concerning the following topics:

- Viewing the routing table
- Determining the gateway of last resort
- Determining the last routing update
- Testing OSI Layer 3 and Layer 7
- Interpreting the **show interface** command
- Clearing interface counters
- Using CDP to troubleshoot
- The **traceroute** command
- The **show controllers** command
- **debug** commands
- Using timestamps
- Enabling the HTTP server
- Using the **netstat** command

Viewing the Routing Table

Router#**show ip route**	Displays entire routing table
Router#**show ip route** *protocol*	Displays table about a specific *protocol* (for example, RIP or IGRP)
Router#**show ip route** *w.x.y.z*	Displays info about route *w.x.y.z*
Router#**show ip route connected**	Displays table of connected routes
Router#**show ip route static**	Displays table of static routes
Router#**show ip route summary**	Displays summary of all routes

Determining the Gateway of Last Resort

`Router(config)#ip default-network` *w.x.y.z*	Sets network *w.x.y.z* to be the default route. All routes not in the routing table will be sent to this network
`Router(config)#ip route 0.0.0.0 0.0.0.0` `172.16.20.1`	Specifies that all routes not in the routing table will be sent to 172.16.20.1

NOTE: You must use the **ip default-network** command with IGRP. Although you can use it with EIGRP or RIP, it is not recommended. Use the **ip route 0.0.0.0 0.0.0.0** command instead.

Routers that use the **ip default-network** command must have either a specific route to that network or a **0.0.0.0 /0** default route.

Determining the Last Routing Update

`Router#show ip route`	Displays the entire routing table
`Router#show ip route` *w.x.y.z*	Displays info about route *w.x.y.z*
`Router#show ip protocols`	Displays IP routing protocol parameters and statistics
`Router#show ip rip database`	Displays the RIP database

OSI Layer 3 Testing

`Router#ping` *w.x.y.z*	Checks for Layer 3 connectivity with device at address *w.x.y.z*
`Router#ping`	Enters extended ping mode, which provides more options

NOTE: See Chapter 20, "ping and traceroute," for all applicable **ping** commands.

OSI Layer 7 Testing

NOTE: See Chapter 19, "Telnet," for all applicable Telnet commands.

Router#**debug telnet**	Displays Telnet negotiation process

Interpreting the show interface Command

Router#**show interface serial 0/0**	Displays status and stats of interface
Serial 0/0 is *up*, line protocol is *up*	First part refers to physical status. Second part refers to logical status
...<output cut>...	
Possible output results:	
Serial 0/0 is *up*, line protocol is *up*	Interface is up and working
Serial 0/0 is *up*, line protocol is *down*	Keepalive or connection problem (no clockrate, bad encapsulation)
Serial 0/0 is *down*, line protocol is *down*	Interface problem, or other end has not been configured
Serial 0/0 is administratively *down*, line protocol is *down*	Interface is disabled— shut down

Clearing Interface Counters

Router#**clear counters**	Resets all interface counters to 0
Router#**clear counters** *interface type/slot*	Resets specific interface counters to 0

Using CDP to Troubleshoot

NOTE: See Chapter 9, "Telnet," for all applicable CDP commands.

traceroute Command

Router#**trace** *w.x.y.z*	Displays all routes used to reach the destination of *w.x.y.z*

See Chapter 20 for all applicable **traceroute** commands.

show controllers Command

Router#**show controllers serial 0/0**	Displays the type of cable plugged into the serial interface (DCE or DTE) and what the clock rate is, if it was set

debug Commands

Router#**debug all**	Turns on all possible debugging
Router#**u all** (short form of **undebug all**)	Turns off all possible debugging
Router#**show debug**	Lists what **debug** commands are on
Router#**terminal monitor**	Debug output will now be seen through a Telnet session (default is to only send output on Console screen)

CAUTION: Turning all possible debugging on is extremely CPU intensive, and will probably cause your router to crash. Use *extreme caution* if you try this on a production device. Instead, be selective in which **debug** commands you turn on.

Do not leave debugging turned on. After you have gathered the necessary information from debugging, turn all debugging off. If you wish to turn off only one specific **debug** command and leave others on, issue the **no debug** *x* command, where *x* is the specific **debug** command you want to disable.

Using Timestamps

`Router(config)#service timestamps`	Adds a timestamp to all system logging messages
`Router(config)#service timestamps debug`	Adds a timestamp to all debugging messages
`Router(config)#service timestamps debug uptime`	Adds a timestamp along with total uptime of router to all debugging messages
`Router(config)#service timestamps debug datetime localtime`	Adds a timestamp displaying local time and date to all debugging messages
`Router(config)#no service timestamps`	Disables all timestamps

TIP: Make sure you have the date and time set with the **clock** command at privileged mode so that the timestamps are more meaningful.

OS IP Verification Commands

The following are commands that you should use to verify what your IP settings are. Different operating systems have different commands.

- **ipconfig** (Windows 2000/XP):

  Click **Start > Run > Command > ipconfig** or **ipconfig/all** .

- **winipcfg** (Windows 95/98/Me):

  Click **Start > Run > winipcfg**.

- **ifconfig** (Mac/Linux):

  #ifconfig

ip http server Command

Router(config)#ip http server	Enables the HTTP server, including the Cisco web browser user interface
Router(config-if)#no ip http server	Disables the HTTP server

> **CAUTION:**   The HTTP server was introduced in Cisco IOS Software Release 11.0 to extend router management to the web. You have limited management capabilities to your router through a web browser if the **ip http server** command is turned on.
>
> Do not turn on the **ip http server** command unless you plan on using the browser interface for the router. Having it on creates a potential security hole, because another port is open.

netstat Command

C\>netstat	Used in Windows and UNIX/Linux to display TCP/IP connection and protocol information. Used at the command prompt in Windows

PART VII

Managing IP Services

Chapter 23   NAT

Chapter 24   DHCP

NAT

This chapter provides information and commands concerning the following topics:

- Configuring dynamic NAT
- Configuring PAT
- Configuring static NAT
- Verifying NAT and PAT configuration
- Troubleshooting NAT and PAT configuration

The following table lists the address ranges as specified in RFC 1918 that can be used by anyone as internal private addresses. These will be your "inside-the-LAN" addresses that will have to be translated into public addresses that can be routed across the Internet. Any network is allowed to use these addresses; however, these addresses are not allowed to be routed onto the public Internet.

Private Addresses		
Class	**RFC 1918 Internal Address Range**	**CIDR Prefix**
A	10.0.0.0–10.255.255.255	10.0.0.0/8
B	172.16.0.0–172.31.255.255	172.16.0.0/12
C	192.168.0.0–192.168.255.255	192.168.0.0/16

Configuring Dynamic NAT: One Private to One Public Address Translation

NOTE: For a complete configuration of NAT/PAT with a diagram for visual assistance, see the sample configuration at the end of this chapter.

Step 1: Define a static route on the remote router stating where public addresses should be routed.	```ISP(config)#ip route 64.64.64.64 255.255.255.255.128 s0/0```	Informs the ISP router where to send packets with addresses destined for 64.64.64.64 255.255.255.255.128
Step 2: Define a pool of usable public IP addresses on your router that will perform NAT.		Private address will receive first available public address in pool
	```Corp(config)#ip nat pool scott 64.64.64.70 64.64.64.126 netmask 255.255.255.128```	Defines the following: • Name of pool is **scott** (The name of the pool can be anything.) • Start of pool is **64.64.64.70** • End of pool is **64.64.64.126** • Subnet mask is **255.255.255.128**
Step 3: Create an ACL that will identify which private IP addresses will be translated.	```Corp(config)#access-list 1 permit 172.16.10.0 0.0.0.255```	
Step 4: Link the access control list (ACL) to the pool of addresses. (Create the translation.)	```Corp(config)#ip nat inside source list 1 pool scott```	Defines the following: • The source of the private addresses is from ACL 1 • The pool of available public addresses is named **scott**
Step 5: Define which interfaces are inside (contain the private addresses).	```Router(config)#int fa 0/0```	
	```Router(config-if)#ip nat inside```	You can have more than one inside interface on a router. Addresses from each inside interface are then allowed to be translated into a public address

| Step 6: Define the outside interface (the interface leading to the public network). | `Router(config)#int s 0/0` | |
| | `Router(config-if)#ip nat outside` | |

Configuring PAT: Many Private to One Public Address Translation

Private addresses all use a single public IP address and numerous port numbers for translation.

Step 1: Define a static route on the remote router stating where public addresses should be routed.	`ISP(config)#ip route 64.64.64.64 255.255.255.255.128 s0/0`	Informs the ISP where to send packets with addresses destined for 64.64.64.64 255.255.255.128
Step 2: Define a pool of usable public IP addresses on your router that will perform NAT (optional).		Use this step if you have many private addresses to translate. A single public IP address can handle thousands of private addresses. Without using a pool of addresses, you can translate all private addresses into the IP address of the exit interface—the serial link to the ISP, for example
	`Corp(config)#ip nat pool scott 64.64.64.70 64.64.64.70 netmask 255.255.255.128`	Defines the following: • Name of pool is **scott** (The name of the pool can be anything.) • Start of pool is **64.64.64.70** • End of pool is **64.64.64.70** • Subnet mask is **255.255.255.128**

Step 3: Create an ACL that will identify which private IP addresses will be translated.	`Corp(config)#access-list 1 permit 172.16.10.0 0.0.0.255`	
Step 4 (Option 1): Link the ACL to the outside public interface. (Create the translation.)	`Corp(config)#ip nat inside source list 1 interface serial 0/0 overload`	The source of the private addresses is from ACL 1 The public address to be translated into is the one assigned to Serial 0/0 The **overload** keyword states that port numbers will be used to handle many translations
Step 4 (Option 2): Link the ACL to the pool of addresses. (Create the translation.)		If using the pool created in Step 1
	`Corp(config)#ip nat inside source list 1 pool scott overload`	The source of the private addresses is from ACL 1 The pool of available addresses is named **scott** The **overload** keyword states that port numbers will be used to handle many translations
Step 5: Define which interfaces are inside (contain the private addresses).	`Corp(config)#int fa 0/0`	
	`Corp(config-if)#ip nat inside`	You can have more than one inside interface on a router
Step 6: Define the outside interface (the interface leading to the public network).	`Corp(config)#int s 0/0`	
	`Corp(config-if)#ip nat outside`	Defines which interface is the outside interface for NAT translation

NOTE: You can have an ip nat pool of more than one address, if needed. The syntax for this is Corp(config)#ip nat pool scott 64.64.64.70 74.64.64.128 netmask 255.255.255.128. You would then have a pool of 63 addresses (and all of their ports) available for translation.

Configuring Static NAT: One Private to One Permanent Public Address Translation

Step 1: Define a static route on the remote router stating where public addresses should be routed.	ISP(config)#ip route 64.64.64.64 255.255.255.255.128 s0/0	Informs the ISP where to send packets with addresses destined for 64.64.64.64 255.255.255.128
Step 2: Create a static mapping on your router that will perform NAT.	Corp(config)#ip nat inside source static 172.16.10.5 64.64.64.65	Permanently translates inside address of 172.16.10.5 to a public address of 64.64.64.65 Use the command for each of the private IP addresses you want to statically map to a public address
Step 3: Define which interfaces are inside (contain the private addresses).	Corp(config)#int fa 0/0	
	Corp(config-if)#ip nat inside	You can have more than one inside interface on a router
Step 4: Define the outside interface (the interface leading to the public network).	Corp(config)#int s 0/0	
	Corp(config-if)#ip nat outside	Defines which interface is the outside interface for NAT translation

CAUTION: Make sure that you have in your router configurations a way for packets to travel back to your NAT router. Include a static route on the ISP router advertising your NAT pool and how to travel back to your internal network. Without this in place, a packet can leave your network with a public address, but will not be able to return if your ISP router does not know where the pool of public addresses exists in the network. You should be advertising the pool of public addresses, not your private addresses.

Verifying NAT and PAT Configuration

Router#**show ip nat translations**	Displays translation table
Router#**show ip nat statistics**	Displays NAT statistics
Router#**clear ip nat translations inside** *a.b.c.d* **outside** *e.f.g.h*	Clears a specific translation from the table before it times out
Router#**clear ip nat translations ***	Clears the entire translation table before entries time out

Troubleshooting NAT and PAT Configuration

Router#**debug ip nat**	Displays information about every packet that is translated Be careful with this command. The router's CPU might not be able to handle this amount of output and might therefore hang the system
Router#**debug ip nat detailed**	Displays greater detail about packets being translated

Configuration Example: Port Address Translation

Figure 23-1 shows the network topology for the PAT configuration that follows using the commands covered in this chapter.

Figure 23-1   Port Address Translation Configuration

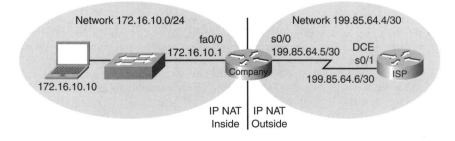

ISP Router

router>**en**	
router#**config t**	
router(config)#**host ISP**	Sets host name
ISP(config)#**no ip domain-lookup**	Turns off DNS resolution to avoid wait time due to DNS lookup of spelling errors
ISP(config)#**enable secret cisco**	Sets encrypted password
ISP(config)#**line con 0**	
ISP(config-line)#**login**	
ISP(config-line)#**password class**	Sets console line password to **class**
ISP(config-line)#**logging synchronous**	Commands will be appended to a new line
ISP(config-line)#**exit**	
ISP(config)#**int s 0/1**	
ISP(config-if)#**ip address 199.85.64.6 255.255.255.252**	Assigns IP address
ISP(config-if)#**clockrate 56000**	Assigns clock rate to data communications equipment (DCE) cable on this side of link
ISP(config-if)#**no shut**	
ISP(config-if)#**int lo0**	Creates loopback interface 0
ISP(config-if)#**ip address 200.200.200.1 255.255.255.255**	Assigns IP address
ISP(config-if)#**exit**	
ISP(config)#**exit**	
ISP#**copy run start**	Saves config to NVRAM

Company Router

`router>en`	
`router#config t`	
`router(config)#host Company`	Sets host name
`Company(config)#no ip domain-lookup`	Turns off DNS resolution to avoid wait time due to DNS lookup of spelling errors
`Company(config)#enable secret cisco`	Sets secret password
`Company(config)#line con 0`	
`Company(config-line)#login`	
`Company(config-line)#password class`	Sets console line password to class
`Company(config-line)#logging synchronous`	Commands will be appended to a new line
`Company(config-line)#exit`	
`Company(config)#int fa 0/0`	
`Company(config-if)#ip address 172.16.10.1 255.255.255.0`	
`Company(config-if)#no shut`	
`Company(config-if)#int s0/0`	
`Company(config-if)#ip add 199.85.64.5 255.255.255.252`	
`Company(config-if)#no shut`	
`Company(config-if)#exit`	
`Company(config)#ip route 0.0.0.0 0.0.0.0 199.85.64.6`	Sends all packets not defined in the routing table to the ISP router
`Company(config)#access-list 1 permit 172.16.10.0 0.0.0.255`	Defines which addresses are permitted through—these addresses are those that will be allowed to be translated with NAT
`Company(config)#ip nat inside source list 1 int s 0/0 overload`	Creates NAT by combining List 1 with the interface S0/0. Overloading will take place

Company(config)#**int fa 0/0**	
Company(config-if)#**ip nat inside**	Location of private inside addresses
Company(config-if)#**int s 0/0**	
Company(config-if)#**ip nat outside**	Location of public outside addresses
Company(config-if)#Ctrl z	
Company#**copy run start**	

CHAPTER 24

DHCP

This chapter provides information and commands concerning the following topics:

- Configuring DHCP
- Verifying and troubleshooting DHCP configuration
- Configuring a DHCP helper address

Configuring DHCP

`Router(config)#ip dhcp pool academy`	Creates a DHCP pool called academy
`Router(dhcp-config)#network 172.16.10.0 255.255.255.0`	Defines the range of addresses to be leased
`Router(dhcp-config)#default-router 172.16.10.1`	Defines the address of the default router for the client
`Router(dhcp-config)#dns-server 172.16.10.10`	Defines the address of the DNS server for the client
`Router(dhcp-config)#netbios-name-server 172.16.10.10`	Defines the address of the NetBIOS server for the client
`Router(dhcp-config)#domain-name empson.ca`	Defines the domain name for the client
`Router(dhcp-config)#lease 14 12 23`	Defines the lease time to be 14 days, 12 hours, 23 minutes
`Router(dhcp-config)#lease infinite`	Sets the lease time to infinity (default time is 1 day)
`Router(dhcp-config)#exit`	
`Router(config)#ip dhcp excluded-address 172.16.10.1 172.16.10.9`	Specifies the range of addresses not to be leased out to clients
`Router(config)#no service dhcp`	Turns the DHCP service off (service is on by default in IOS)
`Router(config)#service dhcp`	Turns the DHCP service on

Verifying and Troubleshooting DHCP Configuration

Router#**show ip dhcp binding**	Displays a list of all bindings created
Router#**show ip dhcp server statistics**	Displays a list of the number of messages sent and received by the DHCP server
Router#**debug ip dhcp server events**	Displays the DHCP process of addresses being leased and returned

Configuring a DHCP Helper Address

Router(config)#**int fa 0/0**	
Router(config-if)#**ip helper-address 172.16.20.2**	Defines that DHCP broadcasts will be forwarded to this specific address rather than be dropped by the router

Configuration Example: DHCP

Figure 24-1   DHCP Configuration

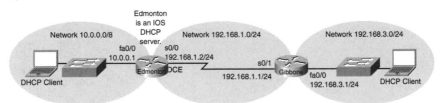

Edmonton Router	
router>**en**	
router#**config t**	
router(config)#**host Edmonton**	Sets hostname
Edmonton(config)#**no ip domain-lookup**	Turns off DNS resolution to avoid wait time due to DNS lookup of spelling errors

`Edmonton(config)#`**`enable secret peace`**	Sets encrypted password to **peace**
`Edmonton(config)#`**`line con 0`**	
`Edmonton(config-line)#`**`login`**	
`Edmonton(config-line)#`**`password class`**	Sets console line password to **class**
`Edmonton(config-line)#`**`logging synchronous`**	Sets commands to be appended to a new line
`Edmonton(config-line)#`**`exit`**	
`Edmonton(config)#`**`int fa 0/0`**	
`Edmonton(config-if)#`**`desc LAN Interface`**	Sets local description of interface
`Edmonton(config-if)#`**`ip address 10.0.0.1 255.0.0.0`**	Assigns IP address
`Edmonton(config-if)#`**`no shut`**	Turns on interface
`Edmonton(config-if)#`**`int serial 0/0`**	
`Edmonton(config-if)#`**`desc Link to Gibbons Router`**	Sets local description of interface
`Edmonton(config-if)#`**`ip address 192.168.1.2 255.255.255.0`**	Assigns IP address
`Edmonton(config-if)#`**`clockrate 56000`**	Assigns clock rate to DCE cable on this side of link
`Edmonton(config-if)#`**`no shut`**	Turns on interface
`Edmonton(config-if)#`**`exit`**	
`Edmonton(config)#`**`router rip`**	Enables RIP routing process
`Edmonton(config-router)#`**`version 2`**	Turns on Version 2
`Edmonton(config-router)#`**`network 10.0.0.0`**	Advertises 10.0.0.0 network
`Edmonton(config-router)#`**`network 192.168.1.0`**	Advertises 192.168.1.0 network
`Edmonton(config-router)#`**`exit`**	

`Edmonton(config)#`**`service dhcp`**	Verifies that router can use DHCP services and that DHCP is enabled
`Edmonton(config)#`**`ip dhcp pool 10network`**	Creates a DHCP pool called **10network**
`Edmonton(dhcp-config)#`**`network 10.0.0.0 255.0.0.0`**	Defines a range of addresses to be leased
`Edmonton(dhcp-config)#`**`default-router 10.0.0.1`**	Defines address of default router for clients
`Edmonton(dhcp-config)#`**`netbios-name-server 10.0.0.2`**	Defines address of NetBIOS WINS server for clients
`Edmonton(dhcp-config)#`**`dns-server 10.0.0.3`**	Defines address of DNS server for clients
`Edmonton(dhcp-config)#`**`domain-name pretenddomain.com`**	Defines domain name for clients
`Edmonton(dhcp-config)#`**`lease 12 14 30`**	Sets lease time to be 12 days, 14 hours, 30 minutes
`Edmonton(dhcp-config)#`**`exit`**	
`Edmonton(config)#`**`ip dhcp excluded-addresses 10.0.0.1 10.0.0.5`**	Specifies range of addresses not to be leased out to clients
`Edmonton(config)#`**`ip dhcp pool 192.168.3network`**	Creates a DHCP pool called **192.168.3network**
`Edmonton(dhcp-config)#`**`network 192.168.3.0 255.255.255.0`**	Defines a range of addresses to be leased
`Edmonton(dhcp-config)#`**`default-router 192.168.3.1`**	Defines address of default router for clients
`Edmonton(dhcp-config)#`**`netbios-name-server 10.0.0.2`**	Defines address of NetBIOS server for clients
`Edmonton(dhcp-config)#`**`dns-server 10.0.0.3`**	Defines address of DNS server for clients
`Edmonton(dhcp-config)#`**`domain-name pretenddomain.com`**	Defines domain name for clients
`Edmonton(dhcp-config)#`**`lease 12 14 30`**	Sets lease time to be 12 days, 14 hours, 30 minutes

`Edmonton(dhcp-config)#`**`exit`**	
`Edmonton(config)#`**`exit`**	
`Edmonton#` **`copy run start`**	Saves config to NVRAM
Gibbons Router	
`router>`**`en`**	
`router#`**`config`** `t`	
`router(config)#`**`host Gibbons`**	Sets hostname
`Gibbons(config)#`**`no ip domain-lookup`**	Turns off DNS resolution to avoid wait time due to DNS lookup of spelling errors
`Gibbons(config)#`**`enable secret love`**	Sets encrypted password to **love**
`Gibbons(config)#`**`line con 0`**	
`Gibbons(config-line)#`**`login`**	
`Gibbons(config-line)#`**`password class`**	Sets console line password to **class**
`Gibbons(config-line)#`**`logging synchronous`**	Sets commands to be appended to a new line
`Gibbons(config-line)#`**`exit`**	
`Gibbons(config)#`**`int fa 0/0`**	
`Gibbons(config-if)#`**`desc LAN Interface`**	Sets local description of interface
`Gibbons(config-if)#`**`ip address 192.168.3.1 255.255.255.0`**	Assigns IP address
`Gibbons(config-if)#`**`ip helper-address 192.168.1.2`**	Defines that UDP broadcasts will be forwarded to this address rather than be dropped
`Gibbons(config-if)#`**`no shut`**	Turns on interface
`Gibbons(config-if)#`**`int serial 0/1`**	

Gibbons(config-if)#**desc Link to Edmonton Router**	Sets local description of interface
Gibbons(config-if)#**ip address 192.168.1.1 255.255.255.0**	Assigns IP address
Gibbons(config-if)#**no shut**	Turns on interface
Gibbons(config-if)#**exit**	
Gibbons(config)#**router rip**	Enables RIP routing process
Gibbons(config-router)#**version 2**	Turns on Version 2
Gibbons(config-router)#**network 192.168.3.0**	Advertises 192.168.3.0 network
Gibbons(config-router)#**network 192.168.1.0**	Advertises 192.168.1.0 network
Gibbons(config-router)#**exit**	
Gibbons(config)#**exit**	
Gibbons#**copy run start**	Saves config to NVRAM

PART VIII

Wide-Area Networks

Chapter 25   HDLC and PPP

Chapter 26   ISDN and DDR

Chapter 27   Frame Relay

HDLC and PPP

This chapter provides information and commands concerning the following Point-to-Point Protocol (PPP) topics:

- Configuring High-Level Data Link Control (HDLC) encapsulation on a serial line
- Configuring PPP on a serial line (mandatory commands)
- Configuring PPP on a serial line (optional commands), including those commands concerning the following:
  - Compression
  - Link quality
  - Multilink
  - Authentication
- Verifying or troubleshooting a serial link/PPP encapsulation

Configuring HDLC Encapsulation on a Serial Line

Router#**config t**	
Router(config)#**int s 0/0**	
Router(config-if)#**encapsulation hdlc**	

NOTE: HDLC is the default encapsulation for synchronous serial links on Cisco routers. You would only use the **encapsulation hdlc** command to return the link back to its default state.

Configuring PPP on a Serial Line (Mandatory Commands)

Router#**config t**	
Router(config)#**int s 0/0**	
Router(config-if)#**encapsulation ppp**	Changes encapsulation from default HDLC to PPP

NOTE: You must execute the **encapsulation ppp** command on both sides of the serial link for the link to become active.

Configuring PPP on a Serial Line (Optional Commands): Compression

`Router(config-if)#compress predictor`	Enables the predictor compression algorithm
`Router(config-if)#compress stac`	Enables the stac compression algorithm

Configuring PPP on a Serial Line (Optional Commands): Link Quality

`Router(config-if)#ppp quality x`	Ensures the link must have a quality of x percent; otherwise, the link will shut down

NOTE: In PPP, the Link Control Protocol allows for an optional link quality determination phase. In this phase, the link is tested to determine whether the link quality is sufficient to bring up any Layer 3 protocols. If you use the command **ppp quality** x, where x is equal to a certain percent, you must meet that percentage of quality on the link. If the link does not meet that percentage level, the link cannot be created and will shut down.

Configuring PPP on a Serial Line (Optional Commands): Multilink

`Router(config-if)#ppp multilink`	Enables load balancing across multiple links

Configuring PPP on a Serial Line (Optional Commands): Authentication

`Router(config)#username routerb password cisco`	Sets a username of **routerb** and a password of **cisco** for authentication from the other side of the PPP serial link. This is used by the local router to authenticate the PPP peer
`Router(config)#int s 0/0`	
`Router(config-if)#ppp authentication pap`	Turns on PAP authentication only

Router(config-if)#`ppp authentication chap`	Turns on CHAP authentication only
Router(config-if)#`ppp authentication pap chap`	Defines that the link will use PAP authentication, but will try CHAP if PAP fails or is rejected by other side
Router(config-if)#`ppp authentication chap pap`	Defines that the link will use CHAP authentication, but will try PAP if CHAP fails or is rejected by other side
Router(config-if)#`ppp pap sent-username routerb password cisco`	This command must be set if using PAP in Cisco IOS Software Release 11.1 or later

TIP: When setting authentication, make sure that your usernames match the name of the router on the other side of the link, and that the passwords on each router match the other. Usernames and passwords are case sensitive. Consider the following example:

Edmonton(config)#`username Calgary password cisco`	Calgary(config)#`username Edmonton password cisco`
Edmonton(config)#`int s 0/0`	Calgary(config)#`int s 0/0`
Edmonton(config-if)#`encapsulation ppp`	Calgary(config if)#`encapsulation ppp`
Edmonton(config-if)#`ppp authentication chap`	Calgary(config-if)#`ppp authentication chap`

NOTE: Because Password Authentication Protocol (PAP) does not encrypt its password as it is sent across the link, recommended practice is that you use Challenge Handshake Authentication Protocol (CHAP) as your authentication method.

Verifying or Troubleshooting a Serial Link/PPP Encapsulation

Router#**show interfaces serial** *x*	Lists info for serial interface *x*
Router#**show controllers serial** *x*	Tells you what type of cable (DCE/DTE) is plugged into your interface and whether a clock rate has been set
Router#**debug serial interface**	Displays whether serial keepalive counters are incrementing
Router#**debug ppp**	Displays any traffic related to PPP
Router#**debug ppp packet**	Displays PPP packets that are being sent and received
Router#**debug ppp negotiation**	Displays PPP packets related to the negotiation of the PPP link
Router#**debug ppp error**	Displays PPP error packets
Router#**debug ppp authentication**	Displays PPP packets related to the authentication of the PPP link
Router#**debug ppp compression**	Displays PPP packets related to the compression of packets across the link

TIP: With frequent lab use, serial cable pins often get bent, which may prevent the router from seeing the cable. The output from the command **show controllers interface serial** *x* will show **no cable** even though a cable is physically present.

Configuration Example: PPP

Figure 25-1 shows the network topology for the configuration that follows, which shows how to configure PPP using the commands covered in this chapter.

Figure 25-1   Network Topology for PPP Configuration

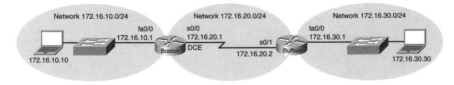

NOTE: The host name, password, and interfaces have all been configured as per the configuration example in Chapter 6, "Configuring a Single Cisco Router."

Boston Router

Boston>**en**	
Boston#**config t**	
Boston(config)#**username Buffalo password academy**	Sets the local username and password for PPP authentication of the PPP peer
Boston(config-if)#**int s 0/0**	
Boston(config-if)#**desc Link to Buffalo Router**	Defines the locally significant link description
Boston(config-if)#**ip add 172.16.20.1 255.255.255.0**	Assigns IP address to interface
Boston(config-if)#**clockrate 56000**	Sets clock rate to data communications equipment (DCE) side of link
Boston(config-if) #**encapsulation ppp**	Turns on PPP encapsulation
Boston(config-if)#**ppp authentication chap**	Turns on CHAP authentication
Boston(config-if)#**no shut**	Turns on interface
Boston(config-if)#**exit**	Exits interface mode
Boston(config)#**exit**	Exits global config mode
Boston#**copy run start**	Saves config to NVRAM

Buffalo Router

Buffalo>**en**	
Buffalo#**config t**	
Buffalo(config)#**username Boston password academy**	Sets username and password for PPP authentication
Buffalo(config-if)#**int s 0/1**	

`Buffalo(config-if)#`**`desc Link to Boston`** **`Router`**	Defines the locally significant link description
`Buffalo(config-if)#`**`ip add 172.16.20.2`** **`255.255.255.0`**	Assigns IP address to interface
`Buffalo(config-if) #`**`encapsulation ppp`**	Turns on PPP encapsulation
`Buffalo(config-if)#`**`ppp authentication`** **`chap`**	Turns on CHAP authentication
`Buffalo(config-if)#`**`no shut`**	Turns on interface
`Buffalo(config-if)#`Ctrl z	Exits back to privileged mode
`Buffalo#`**`copy run start`**	Saves config to NVRAM

CHAPTER 26

ISDN and DDR

This chapter provides information and commands concerning the following topics:

- Setting the switch type in an Integrated Services Digital Network (ISDN) Basic Rate Interface (BRI) configuration
- Setting service profile identifiers (SPIDs) in an ISDN BRI configuration
- Configuring ISDN Primary Rate Interface (PRI)
- Verifying ISDN configuration
- Troubleshooting ISDN
- Configuring legacy dial-on-demand routing (DDR)
- Configuring dialer profiles with DDR

Configuring ISDN BRI: Setting the Switch Type

`Router(config)#isdn switch-type` *switch-type*	Sets the switch type globally for all ISDN interfaces
`Router(config)#int bri 0`	
`Router(config-ifg)#isdn switch-type` *switch-type*	Sets the switch type for this specific interface. Can be different from global switch type if necessary

NOTE: The switch type will be given to you from your service provider.

A main office with 30 branch offices might have 28 offices using one switch type and two offices using a different switch type. Thus, you would use the global-level command to set the switch type to the one required by the 28 offices, and the interface-level command to override this on the two interfaces that needed a different switch type.

Configuring ISDN BRI: Setting SPIDs

Router(config)#**interface bri 0**	
Router(config-if)#**isdn spid1** *51055510000001 5551000*	Defines the SPID number for channel B1, as assigned by the service provider The second number (5551000) is the local dial directory number (LDN), which usually matches the information coming from the ISDN switch
Router(config-if)#**isdn spid2** *51055510010001 5551001*	Defines the SPID number for channel B2, as assigned by the service provider

NOTE: Not all switch types need SPIDs assigned to your router. Your service provider will let you know whether you need to configure SPIDs.

Configuring ISDN PRI

Router(config)#**isdn switch-type** *switch-type*	Same command as with BRI. Can be done globally or in interface config mode
Router(config)#**controller t1 1/0**	Enters into controller config mode where the PRI card is located
Router(config-controller)#**framing** *{sf ¦ esf}*	Sets framing to either Superframe Format (SF) or Extended Superframe Format (ESF) as dictated by the service provider. ESF is the most commonly used framing
Router(config-controller)#**linecode** *{ami ¦ b8zs ¦ hdb3}*	Sets Layer 1 signaling method to alternate mark inversion (AMI), binary 8-zero substitution (B8ZS) or high-density bipolar three (HDB3). B8ZS is used in North America
Router(config-controller)#**pri-group** *timeslots 1-24*	Configures the number of timeslots allocated by the provider, if using a channelized T1 controller
Router(config-controller)#**interface** *serial0/0:23*	Specifies an interface to be used for PRI D-channel operation. This command says to use channel 24 of interface Serial 0/0

NOTE: Channels are numbered starting at zero (0) not one (1). Therefore, the 16th channel would be numbered 15; channel 24 would be numbered 23.

CAUTION: Subinterfaces on a serial interface are shown with a dot (.). Channels are shown with a colon (:). For example,

Serial0/0.23 is subinterface 23.

Serial 0/0:23 is channel 23.

Verifying ISDN Configuration

Router#**show isdn status**	Confirms BRI operations
Router#**show isdn active**	Displays current call information
Router#**show dialer**	Displays information about the dialer interface (used in DDR)
Router#**show interface bri 0/0**	Displays statistics about interface bri 0/0
Router#**show interface bri 0/0:1**	Displays statistics about channel 1 of interface bri 0/0
Router#**clear interface bri 0/0**	Manually resets the interface. All ISDN information will have to be re-sent

TIP: If, after you have set the SPIDs on an interface, the SPIDs have not been sent and verified by the ISDN switch, issue a **clear interface bri 0/0** (or **bri 0**) command to force the router to renegotiate ISDN info with the switch. You might need to issue the **clear interface command** three or four times for the interface to come up.

Troubleshooting ISDN

Router#**debug isdn q921**	Displays info about Layer 2 (data link layer) access taking place on the D channel
Router#**debug isdn q931**	Displays info about Layer 3 (network layer) call setup and teardown between your router and the service provider switch
Router#**debug dialer events**	Displays messages when the DDR link has connected and what traffic caused it to connect
Router#**debug dialer packets**	Displays a message every time a packet is sent out the DDR interface

NOTE: PPP is often used as an encapsulation method when working with ISDN. Therefore, the PPP configuration commands, along with the PPP **debug** commands are applicable here, too.

Configuring Legacy DDR

Step 1: Configure static routes on router.		Using static routes instead of dynamic routing will save on ISDN costs. The link will not always be up because routing updates trigger link to become active
	`Edmonton#`**`config t`**	
	`Edmonton(config)#`**`ip route`** **`172.16.30.2 255.255.255.0`** **`172.16.20.2`**	
Step 2 (Option 1): Define interesting traffic without access lists.		Specifies what type of traffic will trigger the router to make an ISDN call to establish the link
		Tip: The **dialer-list** and **dialer-group** commands can be compared to the **access-list** and **access-group** commands in access control lists (ACLs).
	`Edmonton(config)#`**`dialer-`** **`list 1 protocol ip permit`**	States that all IP traffic is interesting
	`Edmonton(config)#`**`int bri 0`**	
	`Edmonton(config-if)#`**`dialer-`** **`group 1`**	Groups all **dialer-list 1** statements together to apply to this interface
Step 2 (Option 2): Define interesting traffic with access lists (for better control).		Using access lists within dialer lists gives you more control as to what traffic is defined as interesting
	`Edmonton(config)#`**`dialer-`** **`list 2 protocol ip list 150`**	Points dialer list to ACL 150
	`Edmonton(config)#`**`access-`** **`list 150 deny udp any any`** **`eq tftp`**	Denies TFTP traffic

	Edmonton(config)#**access-list 150 deny tcp any any eq telnet**	Denies Telnet traffic
	Edmonton(config)#**access-list 150 permit ip any any**	Permits everything else
	Edmonton(config)#**int bri 0**	
	Edmonton(config-if)#**dialer-group 2**	Groups all **dialer-list 2** statements together on this interface
Step 3: Configure DDR dialer information.		
	Edmonton(config)#**username Calgary password academy**	For PPP encapsulation with authentication across ISDN (optional)
	Edmonton(config)#**int bri 0**	
	Edmonton(config-if)#**encap ppp**	Turns on PPP encapsulation
	Edmonton(config-if)#**ppp authentication chap**	Turns on CHAP authentication
	Edmonton(config-if)#**dialer idle-timeout 150**	Specifies the number of seconds after last interesting traffic is sent before the call terminates. Default is 120 seconds.
	Edmonton(config-if)#**dialer map ip 172.16.20.2 name Calgary 5552000**	Defines the following: • 172.16.20.2 = IP address of next-hop router • Calgary = host name of remote router • 5552000 = number to dial to get there

Configuring Dialer Profiles with DDR

TIP: Using a dial map applies the configuration directly to the interface. Using a dialer profile allows you to have a more dynamic configuration—the physical interface will act differently depending on your specific call requirements, such as the following:

• Do you want HDLC encapsulation instead of PPP?

• Do you want an extended ACL rather than a standard one?

• Do you want a different idle-timeout threshold?

Step 1: Configure static routes on router.		Using static routes rather than dynamic routing will save on ISDN costs. The link will not always be up because routing updates trigger link to remain become active
	`Edmonton#config t`	
	`Edmonton(config)#ip route 172.16.30.0 255.255.255.0 172.16.20.2`	
Step 2 (Option 1): Define interesting traffic without access lists.		
	`Edmonton(config)#dialer-list 1 protocol ip permit`	
	`Edmonton(config)#int dialer 0`	Go to virtual dialer interface as opposed to physical BRI 0 interface
	`Edmonton(config-if)#dialer-group 1`	
Step 2 (Option 2): Define interesting traffic with access lists.		
	`Edmonton(config)#dialer-list 2 protocol ip list 150`	
	`Edmonton(config)#access-list 150 deny udp any any eq tftp`	
	`Edmonton(config)#access-list 150 deny tcp any any eq telnet`	
	`Edmonton(config)#access-list 150 permit ip any any`	
	`Edmonton(config)#int dialer 0`	Go to virtual dialer interface as opposed to physical BRI 0 interface.
	`Edmonton(config-if)#dialer-group 2`	

Step 3: Configure DDR dialer information.		
	`Edmonton(config)#`**`username Calgary password academy`**	For PPP encapsulation across ISDN (optional)
	`Edmonton(config)#`**`int dialer 0`**	
	`Edmonton(config-if)#`**`ip address 172.16.20.1 255.255.255.0`**	
	`Edmonton(config-if)#`**`int bri 0`**	
	`Edmonton(config-if)#`**`encap ppp`**	Turns on PPP encapsulation
	`Edmonton(config-if)#`**`ppp authentication chap`**	Turns on CHAP authentication
	`Edmonton(config-if)#`**`dialer idle-timeout 150`**	Specifies the number of seconds after last interesting traffic is sent before the call terminates. Default is 120 seconds.
Step 4: Configure dialer information.		
	`Edmonton(config)#`**`int dialer 0`**	Enters dialer interface
	`Edmonton(config-if)#`**`dialer remote name Calgary`**	
	`Edmonton(config-if)#`**`dialer string 5552000`**	
Step 5: Associate dialer profile.		
	`Edmonton(config)#`**`interface bri 0`**	
	`Edmonton(config-if)#`**`dialer pool-member 1`**	Or **2** if using **dial-group 2**
	`Edmonton(config-if)#`**`interface dialer 0`**	
	`Edmonton(config-if)#`**`dialer pool 1`**	Or **2** if using **dial-group 2**

Configuration Example: ISDN and DDR with No Dialer Profiles

Figure 26-1 shows the network topology for the ISDN and DDR with no dialer profiles configuration that follows using the commands covered in this chapter.

Figure 26-1   ISDN/DDR with No Dialer Profiles Configuration

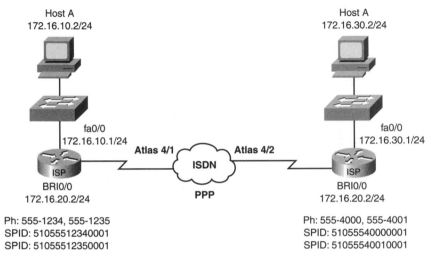

Host A
172.16.10.2/24

Host A
172.16.30.2/24

fa0/0
172.16.10.1/24

fa0/0
172.16.30.1/24

Atlas 4/1   **ISDN**   **Atlas 4/2**

ISP   ISP

BRI0/0   BRI0/0
172.16.20.2/24   **PPP**   172.16.20.2/24

Ph: 555-1234, 555-1235
SPID: 51055512340001
SPID: 51055512350001

Ph: 555-4000, 555-4001
SPID: 51055540000001
SPID: 51055540010001

Edmonton Router

`router>`**`en`**	
`router#`**`config t`**	
`router(config)#`**`host Edmonton`**	Sets host name
`Edmonton(config)#`**`no ip domain-lookup`**	Turns off DNS resolution to avoid wait time due to DNS lookup of spelling errors
`Edmonton(config)#`**`enable secret cisco`**	Sets encrypted password to **cisco**
`Edmonton(config)#`**`line con 0`**	
`Edmonton(config-line)#`**`login`**	
`Edmonton(config-line)#`**`password class`**	Sets console line password to **class**

`Edmonton(config-line)#`**`logging synchronous`**	Returns prompt to same location after info messages interrupt
`Edmonton(config-line)#`**`exit`**	
`Edmonton(config)#`**`int fa 0/0`**	
`Edmonton(config-if)#`**`ip add 172.16.10.1 255.255.255.0`**	Assigns IP address to interface
`Edmonton(config-if)#`**`no shut`**	Turns interface on
`Edmonton(config-if)#`**`exit`**	
`Edmonton(config)#`**`username Calgary password academy`**	For PPP encapsulation across ISDN (optional)
`Edmonton(config)#`**`isdn switch-type basic-ni`**	Sets ISDN switch type for all interfaces to match service provider
`Edmonton(config)#`**`dialer-list 1 protocol ip permit`**	Defines interesting traffic—all IP
`Edmonton(config)#`**`ip route 0.0.0.0 0.0.0.0 172.16.20.2`**	Creates a static route that will send all traffic not defined in the routing table to the next-hop address of 172.16.20.2
`Edmonton(config)#`**`int bri 0/0`**	
`Edmonton(config-if)#`**`ip add 172.16.20.1 255.255.255.0`**	Assigns IP address to interface
`Edmonton(config-if)#`**`encap ppp`**	Turns on PPP encapsulation
`Edmonton(config-if)#`**`ppp authen chap`**	Turns on CHAP authentication
`Edmonton(config-if)#`**`dialer-group 1`**	Assigns traffic from dialer list 1 to this group
`Edmonton(config-if)#`**`isdn spid1 51055512340001 5551234`**	Assigns SPID 1
`Edmonton(config-if)#`**`isdn spid2 51055512350001 5551235`**	Assigns SPID 2
`Edmonton(config-if)#`**`dialer idle-timeout 90`**	Specifies that the interface will disconnect after 90 seconds of no traffic

Edmonton(config-if)#**dialer map ip 172.16.20.2 name Calgary 5554000**	Sets map to find remote router
Edmonton(config-if)#**no shut**	
Edmonton(config-if)#Ctrl z	
Edmonton#**copy run start**	Saves configuration to NVRAM

Calgary Router

router>**en**	
router#**config t**	
router(config)#**host Calgary**	Sets host name
Calgary(config)#**no ip domain-lookup**	Turns off DNS resolution to avoid wait time due to DNS lookup of spelling errors
Calgary(config)#**enable secret cisco**	Sets encrypted password
Calgary(config)#**line con 0**	
Calgary(config-line)#**login**	
Calgary(config-line)#**password console**	Sets console line password
Calgary(config-line)#**logging synchronous**	Returns prompt to same location after info messages interrupt
Calgary(config-line)#**exit**	
Calgary(config)#**int fa 0/0**	
Calgary(config-if)#**ip add 172.16.30.1 255.255.255.0**	Assigns IP address to interface
Calgary(config-if)#**no shut**	Turns interface on
Calgary(config-if)#**exit**	
Calgary(config)#**username Edmonton password academy**	For PPP encapsulation across ISDN (optional)

`Calgary(config)#isdn switch-type basic-ni`	Sets ISDN switch type for all interfaces to match service provider
`Calgary(config)#dialer-list 1 protocol ip permit`	Defines interesting traffic—all IP
`Calgary(config)#ip route 0.0.0.0 0.0.0.0 172.16.20.1`	Creates a static route that will send all traffic not defined in the routing table to the next-hop address of 172.16.20.1
`Calgary(config)#int bri 0/0`	
`Calgary(config-if)#ip add 172.16.20.2 255.255.255.0`	Assigns IP address to interface
`Calgary(config-if)#encap ppp`	Turns on PPP encapsulation
`Calgary(config-if)#ppp authen chap`	Turns on CHAP authentication
`Calgary(config-if)#dialer-group 1`	Assigns traffic from dialer list 1 to this group
`Calgary(config-if)#isdn spid1 51055540000001 5554000`	Assigns SPID 1
`Calgary(config-if)#isdn spid2 51055540010001 5554001`	Assigns SPID 2
`Calgary(config-if)#dialer idle-timeout 60`	Specifies that the interface will disconnect after 60 seconds of no traffic
`Calgary(config-if)#dialer map ip 172.16.20.1 name Edmonton 5551234`	Sets map to find remote router
`Calgary(config-if)#no shut`	
`Calgary(config-if)#`Ctrl z	
`Calgary#copy run start`	Saves configuration to NVRAM

CHAPTER 27

Frame Relay

This chapter provides information and commands concerning the following topics:

- Configuring Frame Relay
  - Setting the encapsulation type
  - Setting the LMI type
  - Setting the DLCI number
  - Configuring a Frame Relay map statement
  - Configuring Frame Relay using subinterfaces
- Verifying Frame Relay
- Troubleshooting Frame Relay

Configuring Frame Relay: Setting the Frame Relay Encapsulation Type

`Router(config)#int s 0/0`	
`Router(config-if)#encapsulation frame-relay`	Turns on Frame Relay encapsulation with the default encapsulation type of **cisco**
or	
`Router(config-if)#encapsulation frame-relay ietf`	Turns on Frame Relay encapsulation with the encapsulation type of **ietf** (RFC 1490). Use the **ietf** encapsulation method if connecting to a non-Cisco router

Configuring Frame Relay: Setting the Frame Relay Encapsulation LMI Type

`Router(config-if)#frame-relay lmi-type {ansi ¦ cisco ¦ q933a}`	Depending on the option you select, this command sets the LMI type to the ANSI standard, the Cisco standard, or the ITU-T Q.933 Annex A standard

NOTE: As of Cisco IOS Software Release 11.2 the LMI type is auto-sensed, making this command optional.

Configuring Frame Relay: Setting the Frame Relay DLCI Number

`Router(config-if)#frame-relay interface-dlci 110`	Sets the DLCI number of 110 on the local interface
`Router(config-fr-dlci)#exit`	
`Router(config)#`	

Configuring a Frame Relay Map

`Router(config-if)#frame-relay map ip 192.168.100.1 110 broadcast`	Maps the remote IP address (192.168.100.1) to the local DLCI number (110)
	The optional **broadcast** keyword specifies that broadcasts across IP should be forwarded to this address. This is necessary when using dynamic routing protocols
`Router(config-if)#no frame-relay inverse arp`	Turns off Inverse ARP

NOTE: Cisco routers have Inverse Address Resolution Protocol (ARP) turned on by default. This means that the router will go out and create the mapping for you. If the remote router does not support Inverse ARP, or you want to control broadcast traffic over the permanent virtual circuit (PVC), you must statically set the DLCI/IP mappings and turn off Inverse ARP.

You need to issue the **no frame-relay inverse-arp** command before you issue the **no shutdown** command; otherwise, the interface performs Inverse ARP before you can turn it off.

Configuring a Description of the Interface (Optional)

Router(config-if)#**description Connection to the Branch office**	Optional command to allow you to enter in additional information such as contact name, PVC description, and so on

Configuring Frame Relay Using Subinterfaces

Subinterfaces enable you to solve split-horizon problems and to create multiple PVCs on a single physical connection to the Frame Relay cloud.

Router(config)#**int s 0/0**	
Router(config-if)#**encapsulation frame-relay ietf**	Sets the Frame Relay encapsulation type for all subinterfaces on this interface
Router(config-if)#**frame-relay lmi-type ansi**	Sets the LMI type for all subinterfaces on this interface
Router(config-if)#**no ip address**	Ensures there is no IP address set to this interface.
Router(config-if)#**no shut**	
Router(config-if)#**interface s 0/0.102 point-to-point**	Creates a point-to-point subinterface numbered 102
Router(config-subif)#**ip address 192.168.10.1 255.255.255.0**	Assigns an IP address to the subinterface
Router(config-subif)#**frame-relay interface-dlci 102**	Assigns a DLCI to the subinterface

`Router(config-subif)#int s 0/0.103 point-to-point`	Creates a point-to-point subinterface numbered 103
`Router(config-subif)#ip address 192.168.20.1 255.255.255.0`	Assigns an IP address to the subinterface
`Router(config-subif)#frame-relay interface-dlci 103`	Assigns a DLCI to the subinterface
`Router(config-subif)#exit`	
`Router(config-if)#exit`	
`Router(config)#`	

NOTE: There are two types of subinterfaces:

- *Point-to-point,* where a single PVC connects one router to another and each sub-interface is in its own IP subnet.
- *Multipoint,* where the router is the middle point of a group of routers. All other routers connect to each other through this router and all routers are in the same subnet.

NOTE: Use the **no ip split-horizon** command to turn off split-horizon commands on multipoint interfaces so that remote sites can see each other.

Verifying Frame Relay

`Router#show frame-relay map`	Displays IP/DLCI map entries
`Router#show frame-relay pvc`	Displays status of all PVCs configured
`Router#show frame-relay lmi`	Displays LMI statistics
`Router#clear frame-relay-inarp`	Clears all Inverse ARP entries from the map table

TIP: If the **clear frame-relay-inarp** command does not clear Frame Relay maps, you might need to reload the router.

Troubleshooting Frame Relay

`Router#debug frame-relay lmi`	Used to help determine whether a router and Frame Relay switch are exchanging LMI packets properly

Configuration Example: Frame Relay

NOTE: For more examples of Frame Relay configurations, I highly recommend Wendell Odom's book *CCNA Self Study: CCNA ICND Exam Certification Guide*, Cisco Press, ISBN 1-58720-083-x. In that book Odom has several different configurations setting up Frame Relay.

Figure 27-1 shows the network topology for the Frame Relay configuration that follows using the commands covered in this chapter.

Figure 27-1   Frame Relay Network

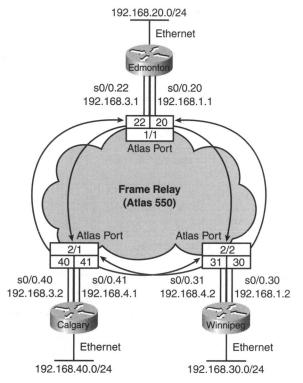

NOTE: For this diagram I am using an Adtran Atlas 550 Device to simulate my Frame Relay cloud. I am using three physical ports (1/1, 2/1, and 2/2) to interconnect my three cities.

Edmonton Router

router>**en**	
router#**config t**	

`router(config)#host Edmonton`	Sets the host name
`Edmonton(config)#no ip domain-lookup`	Turns off DNS queries so that spelling mistakes will not slow you down
`Edmonton(config)#enable secret cisco`	Sets the encrypted password
`Edmonton(config)#line con 0`	
`Edmonton(config-line)#login`	
`Edmonton(config-line)#password class`	Sets console line password to **class**
`Edmonton(config-line)#logging synchronous`	Command being entered will be appended to a new line
`Edmonton(config-line)#exit`	
`Edmonton(config)#int fa 0/0`	
`Edmonton(config-if)#ip address 192.168.20.1 255.255.255.0`	Assigns IP address
`Edmonton(config-if)#no shut`	
`Edmonton(config-if)#int s 0/0`	
`Edmonton(config-if)#encapsulation frame-relay`	Turns on Frame Relay encapsulation
`Edmonton(config-if)#no shut`	
`Edmonton(config-if)#int s0/0.20 point-to-point`	Creates subinterface 20
`Edmonton(config-subif)#desc link to Winnipeg router DLCI 20`	
`Edmonton(config-subif)#ip address 192.168.1.1 255.255.255.0`	Assigns an IP address
`Edmonton(config-subif)#frame-relay interface-dlci 20`	Assigns a DLCI number
`Edmonton(config-subif)#interface s 0/0.22`	Creates subinterface 22
`Edmonton(config-subif)#desc link to Calgary router DLCI 22`	

Edmonton(config-subif)#**ip address 192.168.3.1 255.255.255.0**	Assigns an IP address
Edmonton(config-subif)#**frame-relay interface dlci 22**	Assigns a DLCI number
Edmonton(config-subif)#**exit**	
Edmonton(config-if)#**exit**	
Edmonton(config)#**router eigrp 100**	Turns on the EIGRP routing process 100
Edmonton(config-router)#**network 192.168.1.0**	Advertises network 192.168.1.0, which connects to Winnipeg
Edmonton(config-router)#**network 192.168.3.0**	Advertises network 192.168.3.0, which connects to Calgary
Edmonton(config-router)#**network 192.168.20.0**	Advertises network 192.168.20.0, which is directly connected to local FA 0/interface
Edmonton(config-router)#Ctrl z	
Edmonton#**copy run start**	Saves the configuration to NVRAM

Winnipeg Router

router>**en**	
router#**config t**	
router(config)#**host Winnipeg**	Sets the host name
Winnipeg(config)#**no ip domain-lookup**	Turns off DNS queries so that spelling mistakes will not slow you down
Winnipeg(config)#**enable secret cisco**	Sets the encrypted password to **cisco**
Winnipeg(config)#**line con 0**	

`Winnipeg(config-line)#`**`login`**	
`Winnipeg(config-line)#`**`password class`**	Sets the console line password to **class**
`Winnipeg(config-line)#`**`logging synchronous`**	Command being entered will be appended to a new line
`Winnipeg(config-line)#`**`exit`**	
`Winnipeg(config)#`**`int fa 0/0`**	
`Winnipeg(config-if)#`**`ip address 192.168.30.1 255.255.255.0`**	Assigns an IP address
`Winnipeg(config-if)#`**`no shut`**	
`Winnipeg(config-if)#`**`int s 0/0`**	
`Winnipeg(config-if)#`**`encapsulation frame-relay`**	Turns on Frame Relay encapsulation
`Winnipeg(config-if)#`**`no shut`**	
`Winnipeg(config-if)#`**`int s0/0.30 point-to-point`**	Creates subinterface 30
`Winnipeg(config-subif)#`**`desc link to Edmonton router DLCI 30`**	
`Winnipeg(config-subif)#`**`ip address 192.168.1.2 255.255.255.0`**	Assigns an IP address
`Winnipeg(config-subif)#`**`frame-relay interface-dlci 30`**	Assigns a DLCI number
`Winnipeg(config-subif)#`**`interface s 0/0.31`**	Creates subinterface 31
`Winnipeg(config-subif)#`**`desc link to Calgary router DLCI 31`**	
`Winnipeg(config-subif)#`**`ip address 192.168.4.2 255.255.255.0`**	Assigns an IP address
`Winnipeg(config-subif)#`**`frame-relay interface-dlci 31`**	Assigns a DLCI number
`Winnipeg(config-subif)#`**`exit`**	
`Winnipeg(config-if)#`**`exit`**	

`Winnipeg(config)#`**`router eigrp 100`**	Turns on EIGRP routing process 100
`Winnipeg(config-router)#`**`network 192.168.1.0`**	Advertises network 192.168.1.0 (to Winnipeg)
`Winnipeg(config-router)#`**`network 192.168.4.0`**	Advertises network 192.168.4.0 (to Calgary)
`Winnipeg(config-router)#`**`network 192.168.30.0`**	Advertises network 192.168.30.0 directly connected to FA 0/0
`Winnipeg(config-router)#`Ctrl z	
`Winnipeg#`**`copy run start`**	Saves the configuration to NVRAM

Calgary Router

`router>`**`en`**	
`router#`**`config t`**	
`router(config)#`**`host Calgary`**	Sets the host name
`Calgary(config)#`**`no ip domain-lookup`**	Turns off DNS queries so that spelling mistakes will not slow you down
`Calgary(config)#`**`enable secret cisco`**	Sets the encrypted password to **cisco**
`Calgary(config)#`**`line con 0`**	
`Calgary(config-line)#`**`login`**	
`Calgary(config-line)#`**`password class`**	Sets the console line password to **class**
`Calgary(config-line)#`**`logging synchronous`**	Command being entered will be appended to a new line
`Calgary(config-line)#`**`exit`**	
`Calgary(config)#`**`int fa 0/0`**	

`Calgary(config-if)#ip address 192.168.40.1 255.255.255.0`	Assigns an IP address
`Calgary(config-if)#no shut`	
`Calgary(config-if)#int s 0/0`	
`Calgary(config-if)#encapsulation frame-relay`	Turns on Frame Relay encapsulation
`Calgary(config-if)#no shut`	
`Calgary(config-if)#int s0/0.40 point-to-point`	Creates subinterface 40
`Calgary(config-subif)#desc link to Edmonton router DLCI 40`	
`Calgary(config-subif)#ip address 192.168.3.2 255.255.255.0`	Assigns an IP address
`Calgary(config-subif)#frame-relay interface-dlci 40`	Assigns a DLCI number
`Calgary(config-subif)#interface s 0/0.41`	Creates subinterface 41
`Calgary(config-subif)#desc link to Winnipeg router DLCI 41`	
`Calgary(config-subif)#ip address 192.168.4.1 255.255.255.0`	Assigns an IP address
`Calgary(config-subif)#frame-relay interface-dlci 41`	Assigns a DLCI number
`Calgary(config-subif)#exit`	
`Calgary(config-if)#exit`	
`Calgary(config)#router eigrp 100`	Turns on EIGRP routing process 100
`Calgary(config-router)#network 192.168.3.0`	Advertises the network to Winnipeg
`Calgary(config-router)#network 192.168.4.0`	Advertises the network to Calgary
`Calgary(config-router)#network 192.168.40.0`	Advertises the local FA 0/0 network
`Calgary(config-router)#`Ctrl z	
`Calgary#copy run start`	Saves the configuration to NVRAM

PART IX

Network Security

Chapter 28   IP Access Control List Security

IP Access Control List Security

This chapter provides information and commands concerning the following topics:

- The numbers assigned to the different types of access control lists (ACLs)
- The use of wildcard masks in ACLs
- The **any** and **host** keywords used by ACLs
- How to create, apply, verify, and remove standard IP ACLs
- How to create, apply, verify, and remove extended IP ACLs
- How to create named ACLs
- How to restrict virtual terminal access

Access List Numbers

1–99 or 1300–1999	Standard IP
100–199 or 2000–2699	Extended IP
600–699	AppleTalk
800–899	IPX
900–999	Extended IPX
1000–1099	IPX Service Advertising Protocol

ACL Keywords

`any`	Used in place of 0.0.0.0 255.255.255.255, will match any address that it is compared against
`host`	Used in place of 0.0.0.0 in the wildcard mask; this will match only one specific address

Creating Standard ACLs

Router(config)#**access-list 10 permit 172.16.0.0 0.0.255.255**	Read this line to say: All packets with a source IP address of 172.16.x.x will be permitted to continue through the internetwork
access-list	ACL command
10	Arbitrary number between 1 and 99, designating this as a standard IP ACL
permit	Packets that match this statement will be allowed to continue
172.16.0.0	Source IP address to be compared to
0.0.255.255	Wildcard mask
Router(config)#**access-list 10 deny host 172.17.0.1**	Read this line to say: All packets with a source IP address of 172.17.0.1 will be dropped and discarded
access-list	ACL command
10	Number between 1 and 99, designating this as a standard IP ACL
deny	Packets that match this statement will be dropped and discarded
host	Keyword
172.17.0.1	Specific host address
Router(config)#**access-list 10 permit any**	Read this line to say: All packets with any source IP address will be permitted to continue through the internetwork

access-list	ACL command
10	Number between 1 and 99, designating this as a standard IP ACL
permit	Packets that match this statement will be allowed to continue
any	Keyword to mean all IP addresses

TIP: There is an **implicit deny** statement that is hard coded into every ACL. You cannot see it, but it states "deny everything not already permitted." This is always the last line of any ACL. If you want to defeat this implicit deny, put a **permit any** statement in your standard ACLs or **permit ip any any** in your extended ACLs as the last line.

Applying a Standard ACL to an Interface

Router(config)#int fa0/0	
Router(config-if)#ip access-group 10 in	Takes all access list lines that are defined as being part of group 10 and applies them in an inbound manner. Packets going into the router from FA0/0 will be checked

TIP: Access lists can be applied in either an inbound direction (keyword **in**) or in an outbound direction (keyword **out**).

Verifying ACLs

Router#show ip interface	Displays any ACLs applied to that interface
Router#show access-lists	Displays contents of all ACLs on the router
Router#show access-list access-list-number	Displays contents of ACL by the number specified

Router#**show access-list** *name*	Displays contents of ACL by the *name* specified
Router#**show run**	Displays all ACLs and interface assignments

Removing an ACL

Router(config)#**no access-list 10**	Removes **all** ACLs numbered 10

Creating Extended ACLs

Router(config)#**access-list 110 permit tcp 172.16.0.0 0.0.0.255 192.168.100.0 0.0.0.255 eq 80**	Read this line to say: HTTP packets with a source IP address of 172.16.0.x will be permitted to travel to destination address of 192.168.100.x
access-list	ACL command
110	Number is between 100 and 199, designating this as an extended IP ACL
permit	Packets that match this statement will be allowed to continue
tcp	Protocol must be TCP
172.16.0.0	Source IP address to be compared to
0.0.0.255	Wildcard mask
192.168.100.0	Destination IP address to be compared to
0.0.0.255	Wildcard mask
eq	Operand, means "equal to"

80	Port 80, indicating HTTP traffic
Router(config)#access-list 110 deny tcp any 192.168.100.7 0.0.0.0 eq 23	Read this line to say: Telnet packets with any source IP address will be dropped if they are addressed to specific host 192.168.100.7
access-list	ACL command
110	Number is between 100 and 199, designating this as an extended IP ACL
deny	Packets that match this statement will be dropped and discarded
tcp	Protocol must be TCP protocol
any	Any source IP address
192.168.100.7	Destination IP address to be compared to
0.0.0.0	Wildcard mask; address must match exactly
eq	Operand, means "equal to"
23	Port 23, indicating Telnet traffic

The established Keyword

Router(config)#access-list 110 permit tcp 172.16.0.0 0.0.0.255 192.168.100.0 0.0.0.255 eq 80 established	Indicates an established connection

> **NOTE:** A match will now occur only if the TCP datagram has the ACK or the RST bit set.

> **TIP:** The **established** keyword will work only for TCP, not UDP

> **TIP:** Consider the following situation: You do not want hackers exploiting port 80 to access your network. Because you do not host a web server, it is possible to block incoming traffic on port 80...except that your internal users need web access. When they request a web page, return traffic on port 80 must be allowed. The solution to this problem is to use the **established** command. The ACL will allow the response to enter your network, as it will have the ACK bit set as a result of the initial request from inside your network. Requests from the outside world will still be blocked, because the ACK bit will not be set, but responses will be allowed through.

Creating Named ACLs

Router(config)#**ip access-list extended serveraccess**	Creates an extended named ACL called serveraccess
Router(config-ext-nacl)#**permit tcp any host 131.108.101.99 eq smtp**	Permits mail packets from any source to reach host 131.108.101.99
Router(config-ext-nacl)#**permit udp any host 131.108.101.99 eq domain**	Permits DNS packets from any source to reach host 131.108.101.99
Router(config-ext-nacl)#**deny ip any any log**	Denies all other packets from going anywhere. If any packets do get denied, then log the results for me to look at later
Router(config-ext-nacl)#**exit**	
Router(config)#**int fa 0/0** Router(config-if)#**ip access-group serveraccess out**	Applies this ACL to the Fast Ethernet interface 0/0 in an outbound direction

Using Sequence Numbers in Named ACLs

`Router(config)#ip access-list extended serveraccess2`	Creates an extended named ACL called **serveraccess2**
`Router(config-ext-nacl)#10 permit tcp any host 131.108.101.99 eq smtp`	Uses a sequence number of **10** for this line
`Router(config-ext-nacl)#20 permit udp any host 131.108.101.99 eq domain`	Sequence number of **20** will be applied after line **10**
`Router(config-ext-nacl)#30 deny ip any any log`	Sequence number **30** will be applied after **20**
`Router(config-ext-nacl)#exit`	
`Router(config)#int fa 0/0`	
`Router(config-if)#ip access-group serveraccess2 out`	Applies this ACL to the FastEthernet Interface 0/0 in an outbound direction
`Router(config-if)#exit`	
`Router(config)#ip access-list extended serveraccess2`	
`Router(config-ext-nacl)#25 permit tcp any host 131.108.101.99 eq ftp`	Sequence number of **25** places this line after line **20** and before line **30**
`Router(config-ext-nacl)#exit`	

TIP: Sequence numbers are used to allow for easier editing of your ACL's. The preceding example used numbers 10, 20, and 30 in the ACL lines. If I needed to add another line to this ACL, it would have previously been added after the last line—my line 30. If I needed a line to go closer to the top, I would have had to remove the entire ACL and then reapply it with the lines in the correct order. Now I can enter in a new line with a sequence number, placing it in the correct location.

NOTE: The *sequence-number* argument was added in IOS version 12.2(14)S. It was integrated into Cisco IOS Software Release 12.2(15)T.

Removing Specific Lines in a Named ACL Using Sequence Numbers

`Router(config)#ip access-list extended serveraccess2`	
`Router(config-ext-nacl)#no 20`	Removes line **20** from the list
`Router(config-ext-nacl)#exit`	

Sequence Number Tips

- Sequence Numbers start at '10' and increment by '10' for each line.
- If you forget to add a sequence number, the line will be added to the end of the list.
- Sequence numbers are **changed on a router reload** to reflect the increment by 10 policy (tip #1). If your ACL had numbers 10, 20, 30, 32, 40, 50, and 60 in it, on reload these numbers would become 10, 20, 30, 40, 50, 60, 70.
- Sequence Numbers cannot be seen when using the Router#**show run** or Router#**show start** command. To see sequence numbers, use one of the following commands:

    `Router#show access-lists`
    `Router#show access-lists list name`
    `Router#show ip access-list`
    `Router#show ip access-list list name`

Including Comments About Entries in ACLs

`Router(config)#access-list 10 remark only Jones has access`	**remark** command allows you to include comment. Limited to 100 characters
`Router(config)#access-list 10 permit 172.16.100.119`	
`Router(config)# ip access-list extended telnetaccess`	
`Router(config-ext-nacl)#remark do not let Smith have telnet`	
`Router(config-ext-nacl)#deny tcp host 172.16.100.153 any eq telnet`	

TIP: You can use the **remark** command in any of the IP numbered standard, IP numbered extended, or named IP ACLs.

TIP: You can use the **remark** command either before or after a **permit** or **deny** statement. Therefore, be consistent in your placement to avoid any confusion as to which line the **remark** statement is referring.

Applying an Extended ACL to an Interface

`Router(config)#int fa0/0`
 	
`Router(config-if)#ip access-group 110 out`
	Takes all access list lines that are defined as being part of group 110 and applies them in an outbound manner. Packets going out FA0/0 will be checked

TIP: Access lists can be applied in either an inbound direction (keyword **in**) or in an outbound direction (keyword **out**).

TIP: Only one access list can be applied per interface, per direction.

Restricting Virtual Terminal Access

`Router(config)#access-list 2 permit host` `172.16.10.2`	Permits host 172.16.10.2 to Telnet into this router (see line 4 of this ACL)
`Router(config)#access-list 2 permit 172.16.20.0` `0.0.0.255`	Permits anyone from the 172.16.20.x address range to Telnet into this router (see line 4 of this ACL)
`Router(config)#line vty 0 4`	Denies all other Telnet requests (because of the implicit deny)
`Router(config-line)access-class 2 in`	Applies this ACL to all five vty virtual interfaces

Configuration Example: Access Control Lists

Figure 28-1 shows the network topology for the configuration that follows, which shows five ACL examples using the commands covered in this chapter.

Figure 28-1   Network Topology for ACL Configuration

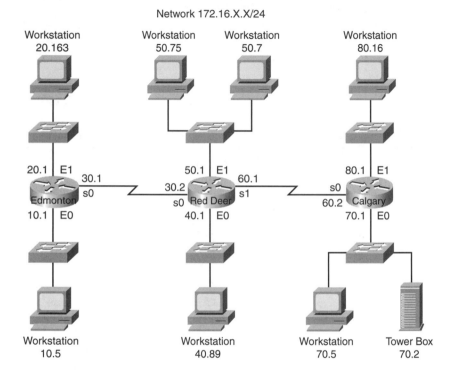

Example 1: Write an ACL that prevents the 10.0 network from accessing the 40.0 network, but everyone else can.

RedDeer(config)#**access-list 10 deny 172.16.10.0 0.0.0.255**	Standard ACL denies complete network for complete TCP/IP suite of protocols
RedDeer(config)#**access-list 10 permit any**	Defeats the implicit deny
RedDeer(config)#**int e0**	
RedDeer(config)#**ip access-group 10 out**	Applies ACL in an outbound direction

Example 2: Write an ACL which states that 10.5 cannot access 50.7. Everyone else can.

Edmonton(config)#**access list 115 deny ip host 172.16.10.5 host 172.16.50.7**	Extended ACL denies specific host for entire TCP/IP suite
Edmonton(config)#**access list 115 permit ip any any**	All others permitted through
Edmonton(config)#**int e0**	
Edmonton(config)#**ip access-group 115 in**	Applies ACL in an inbound direction

Example 3: Write an ACL which states that 10.5 can Telnet to the Red Deer router. No one else can.

RedDeer(config)#**access-list 20 permit host 172.16.10.5**	
RedDeer(config)#**line vty 0 4**	Go to virtual terminal lines
RedDeer(config-line)#**access-class 20 in**	Use **access-class**, not **access-group**

Example 4: Write an ACL which states that 20.163 can Telnet to 70.2. No one else from 20.0 can Telnet to 70.2. Any other host from any other subnet can connect to 70.2 using anything that is available.

Calgary(config)#**access list 150 permit tcp host 172.16.20.163 host 172.16.70.2 eq 23**	
Calgary(config)#**access list 150 deny tcp 172.16.20.0 0.0.0.255 host 172.16.70.2 eq 23**	
Calgary(config)#**access list 150 permit ip any any**	Defeats the implicit deny
Calgary(config)#**int e0**	
Calgary(config)#**ip access-group 150 out**	

Example 5: Write an ACL which states that 50.1–50.63 are not allowed web access to 80.16. Hosts 50.64–50.254 are. Everyone can do everything else.

RedDeer(config)#**access-list 101 deny tcp 172.16.50.0 0.0.0.63 host 172.16.80.16 eq 80**	
RedDeer(config)#**access-list 101 permit ip any any**	Allows device to do everything, including Telnet
RedDeer(config)#**int e1**	
RedDeer(config)#**ip access-group 101 in**	

PART X

Appendixes

Appendix A   Complete Configuration Example

Appendix B   Binary/Hex/Decimal Conversion Chart

Appendix C   Create Your Own Journal Here

Complete Configuration Example

Figure A-1 shows the network topology for the complete configuration that follows.

Figure A-1 Network Topology for Configuration Example

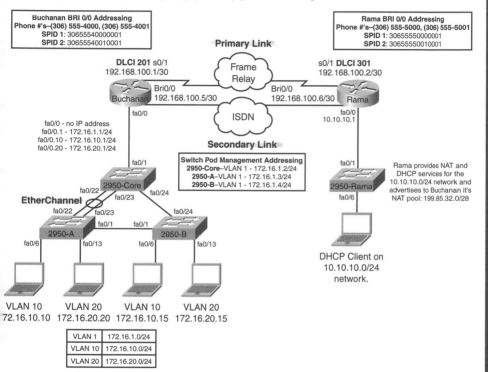

Rama Switch	
switch>**en**	Enters privileged mode
switch#**config t**	Enters global config mode
switch(config)#**no ip domain-lookup**	Turns off DNS queries so that spelling mistakes won't slow you down
switch(config)#**hostname 2950-Rama**	Sets hostname
2950-Rama(config)#**enable secret cisco**	Sets encrypted secret password

2950-Rama(config)#`line con 0`	Enters line console mode
2950-Rama(config-line)#`logging synchronous`	Appends commands to new line so that router information won't interrupt
2950-Rama(config-line)#`login`	User must log in to console before use
2950-Rama(config-line)#`password rooster`	Sets password to **rooster**
2950-Rama(config-line)#`exec-timeout 0 0`	Console will never log out. Note that this is a security risk in a production environment
2950-Rama(config-line)#`exit`	Moves back to global config mode
2950-Rama(config)#`line aux 0`	Moves to line auxiliary mode
2950-Rama(config-line)#`login`	User must log in to auxiliary port before use
2950-Rama(config-line)#`password crows`	Sets password to **crows**
2950-Rama(config-line)#`exit`	Moves back to global config mode
2950-Rama(config)#`line vty 0 15`	Moves to configure all 16 vty ports at same time
2950-Rama(config-line)#`login`	User must log in to vty port before use
2950-Rama(config-line)#`password midnight`	Sets password to **midnight**
2950-Rama(config-line)#`exit`	Exits back to global config mode
2950-Rama(config)#`ip default-gateway 10.10.10.1`	Sets default gateway
2950-Rama(config)#`int vlan 1`	Moves to virtual interface VLAN1
2950-Rama(config-if)#`ip add 10.10.10.2 255.255.255.0`	Sets IP address for switch
2950-Rama(config-if)#`no shut`	Turns virtual interface on
2950-Rama(config-if)#`int fa 0/1`	Moves to interface fa 0/1
2950-Rama(config-if)#`desc Link to Router`	Sets local description
2950-Rama(config-if)#`int fa 0/6`	Moves to interface fa 0/6
2950-Rama(config-if)#`desc Access Link to Client Workstation`	Sets local description
2950-Rama(config-if)#`switchport port-security`	Activates port security

`2950-Rama(config-if)#switchport port-security maximum 1`	Specifies that only one MAC address will be allowed in the MAC table
`2950-Rama(config-if)#switchport port-security violation shutdown`	Sets port to be turned off if more than one MAC address is reported
`2950-Rama(config-if)#exit`	Exits back to global config mode
`2950-Rama(config)#exit`	Returns to privileged mode
`2950-Rama#copy run start`	Saves config to NVRAM
Rama Router	
`Router>en`	Enters privileged mode
`Router#clock set 10:30:00 15 Nov 2005`	Sets local time on router
`Router#config t`	Enters global config mode
`Router(config)#hostname Rama`	Sets router name to Rama
`Rama(config)#no ip domain-lookup`	Turns off DNS queries on unrecognized commands (spelling mistakes)

`Rama(config)#banner motd #`
`This is the Rama Router.`
`Authorized Access Only`
`#`
	Creates an MOTD banner

`Rama(config)#clock timezone CST -6`	Sets time zone to Central Standard Time (6 hours behind UTC)
`Rama(config)#enable secret cisco`	Enable secret password set to **cisco**
`Rama(config)#service password-encryption`	Sets passwords to have weak encryption
`Rama(config)#line con 0`	Enters line console mode
`Rama(config-line)#logging sync`	Commands won't be interrupted by unsolicited messages
`Rama(config-line)#password rooster`	Sets password to **rooster**
`Rama(config-line)#login`	Enables password checking at login
`Rama(config-line)#exec-timeout 0 0`	Console will never log out. Note that this is a security risk in a production environment

`Rama(config-line)#line aux 0`	Moves to line auxiliary mode
`Rama(config-line)#password crows`	Sets password to **crows**
`Rama(config-line)#login`	Enables password checking at login
`Rama(config-line)#line vty 0 4`	Moves to virtual lines zero through four
`Rama(config-line)#password midnight`	Sets password to **midnight**
`Rama(config-line)#login`	Enables password checking at login
`Rama(config-line)#exit`	Moves back to global config mode
`Rama(config)#int fa0/0`	Moves to FastEthernet 0/0
`Rama(config-if)#desc Local LAN`	Sets locally significant description of the interface
`Rama(config-if)#ip address 10.10.10.1 255.255.255.0`	Assigns IP address and subnet mask to interface
`Rama(config-if)#ip nat inside`	Sets location of private inside addresses
`Rama(config-if)#no shut`	Turns on interface
`Rama(config-if)#int s0/1`	Moves directly to Serial 0/1
`Rama(config-if)#desc Primary Link to Buchanan Router`	Sets locally significant description of the interface
`Rama(config-if)#ip address 192.168.100.2 255.255.255.252`	Assigns IP address and subnet mask to interface
`Rama(config-if)#encapsulation frame-relay`	Turns on Frame Relay encapsulation
`Rama(config-if)#frame-relay map ip 192.168.100.1 301 broadcast`	Maps remote IP to local DLCI number, and carries broadcast traffic
`Rama(config-if)#ip nat outside`	Sets location of public outside addresses
`Rama(config-if)#backup interface bri0/0`	Makes ISDN a backup to Frame Relay in event of failure
`Rama(config-if)#backup delay 6 8`	Sets ISDN to take over **6** seconds after S0/0 failure and go down **8** seconds after S0/0 comes back up
`Rama(config-if)#no shut`	Turns on interface
`Rama(config-if)#exit`	Moves back to global config mode
`Rama(config)#isdn switch-type basic-ni`	Sets ISDN switch-type

`Rama(config)#username Buchanan password talktome`	Sets the local username and password for authentication of a PPP peer
`Rama(config)#dialer-list 1 protocol ip permit`	Defines interesting traffic that will trigger an ISDN call
`Rama(config)#interface bri0/0`	Moves to BRI Interface mode
`Rama(config-if)#desc Backup Link to Buchanan Router`	Sets locally significant description of the interface
`Rama(config-if)#ip address 192.168.100.6 255.255.255.252`	Assigns IP address and subnet mask to interface
`Rama(config-if)#encapsulation ppp`	Turns on PPP encapsulation
`Rama(config-if)#ppp authentication chap`	Turns on CHAP authentication
`Rama(config-if)#isdn spid1 30655550000001 5555000`	Assigns SPID for channel B1
`Rama(config-if)#isdn spid 2 30655550010001 5555001`	Assigns SPID for channel B2
`Rama(config-if)#dialer map ip 192.168.100.5 name Buchanan broadcast 5554000`	Sets map to find remote router
`Rama(config-if)#dialer idle-timeout 60`	Sets interface to disconnect after 60 seconds of no traffic
`Rama(config-if)#dialer-group 1`	Assigns traffic filtered by dialer-list 1 to this group
`Rama(config-if)#ip nat outside`	Sets location of public outside addresses
`Rama(config-if)#exit`	Returns to global config mode
`Rama(config)#access-list 1 permit 10.10.10.0 0.0.0.255`	Defines which addresses will be allowed to be translated with NAT
`Rama(config)# ip nat pool rama 199.85.32.1 199.85.32.14 netmask 255.255.255.240`	Creates a pool of public addresses that will be used for NAT
`Rama(config)#ip nat inside source list 1 pool rama overload`	Creates NAT by combining Access List 1 with pool of public addresses called rama. PAT (Overloading) will take place
`Rama(config)#service dhcp`	Verifies that router can use DHCP services and that DHCP is enabled

`Rama(config)#ip dhcp pool 10network`	Creates a DHCP pool called **10network** for the 10.10.10.0 network
`Rama(dhcp-config)#network 10.10.10.0 255.255.255.0`	Defines range of addresses to be leased
`Rama(dhcp-config)#default-router 10.0.0.1`	Defines address of default router for clients
`Rama(dhcp-config)#netbios-name-server 10.0.0.5`	Defines address of NetBIOS server for clients
`Rama(dhcp-config)#dns-server 10.0.0.6`	Defines address of DNS server for clients
`Rama(dhcp-config)#domain-name example.com`	Defines domain name for clients
`Rama(dhcp-config)#lease 12 14 30`	Sets lease time to be 12 days, 14 hours, 30 minutes
`Rama(dhcp-config)#exit`	Returns to global config mode
`Rama(config)#ip dhcp excluded addresses 10.0.0.1 10.0.0.10`	Specifies range of addresses not to be leased out to clients
`Rama(config)#ip host Buchanan 192.168.100.1 192.168.100.5`	Sets a local host name resolution to IP address 192.168.100.1 or 192.168.100.5
`Rama(config)#ip route 0.0.0.0 0.0.0.0 192.168.100.1`	Defines that all traffic not in local table will be routed to address 192.168.100.1 (across Frame Relay Link)
`Rama(config)#ip route 0.0.0.0 0.0.0.0 192.168.100.5 225`	Creates a floating static route to send traffic across ISDN link if Frame Relay network goes down
`Rama(config)#exit`	Moves back to privileged mode
`Rama#copy run start`	Saves config to NVRAM
Buchanan Router	
`Router>en`	Enters privileged mode
`Router#clock set 10:45:00 15 Nov 2005`	Sets local time on router
`Router#config t`	Enters global config mode
`Router(config)#hostname Buchanan`	Sets router name to **Buchanan**

`Buchanan(config)#no ip domain-lookup`	Turns off DNS queries on unrecognized commands (spelling mistakes)

`Buchanan(config)#banner motd #`
`This is the Buchanan Router.`
`Authorized Access Only`
`#`
	Creates an MOTD banner

`Buchanan(config)#clock timezone CST -6`	Sets time zone to Central Standard Time (6 hours behind UTC)
`Buchanan(config)#enable secret cisco`	Enables secret password set to **cisco**
`Buchanan(config)#service password-` `encryption`	Sets passwords to have weak encryption
`Buchanan(config)#line con 0`	Enters line console mode
`Buchanan(config-line)#logging sync`	Sets commands to be appended to a new line
`Buchanan(config-line)#password rooster`	Sets password to **rooster**
`Buchanan(config-line)#login`	Enables password checking at login
`Buchanan(config-line)#exec-timeout 0 0`	Console will never log out. Note that this is a security risk in a production environment
`Buchanan(config-line)#line aux 0`	Moves to line auxiliary mode
`Buchanan(config-line)#password crows`	Sets password to **crows**
`Buchanan(config-line)#login`	Enables password checking at login
`Buchanan(config-line)#line vty 0 4`	Moves to vty zero through four
`Buchanan(config-line)#password midnight`	Sets password to **midnight**
`Buchanan(config-line)#login`	Enables password checking at login
`Buchanan(config-line)#exit`	Moves back to global config mode
`Buchanan(config)#int s0/1`	Moves to S0/0 mode
`Buchanan(config-if)#desc Primary Link to` `Rama Router`	Sets locally significant description of the interface
`Buchanan(config-if)#ip address` `192.168.100.1 255.255.255.252`	Assigns IP address and subnet mask to interface
`Buchanan(config-if)#encapsulation frame-` `relay`	Turns on Frame Relay encapsulation

Buchanan(config-if)#frame-relay map ip 192.168.100.2 201 broadcast	Maps remote IP to local DLCI number
Buchanan(config-if)#backup interface bri0/0	Designates ISDN as a backup interface to Frame Relay in event of failure
Buchanan(config-if)#backup delay 6 8	Sets ISDN to take over 6 seconds after S0/0 failure and goes down 8 seconds after S0/0 comes back up
Buchanan(config-if)#no shut	Turns on interface
Buchanan(config-if)#exit	Moves back to global config mode
Buchanan(config)#isdn switch-type basic-ni	Sets ISDN switch type
Buchanan(config)#username Rama password talktome	Sets the local username and password for authentication of a PPP peer
Buchanan(config)#dialer-list 1 protocol ip permit	Defines interesting traffic that will trigger an ISDN call
Buchanan(config)#interface bri0/0	Moves to BRI mode
Buchanan(config-if)#desc Backup Link to Rama Router	Sets locally significant description of the interface
Buchanan(config-if)#ip address 192.168.100.5 255.255.255.252	Assigns IP address and subnet mask to interface
Buchanan(config-if)#encapsulation ppp	Turns on PPP encapsulation
Buchanan(config-if)#ppp authentication chap	Turns on CHAP authentication
Buchanan(config-if)#isdn spid1 30655540000001 5554000	Assigns SPID for channel B1
Buchanan(config-if)#isdn spid 2 30655540010001 5554001	Assigns SPID for channel B2
Buchanan(config-if)#dialer map ip 192.168.100.6 name Rama broadcast 5555000	Sets map to find remote router
Buchanan(config-if)#dialer idle-timeout 60	Sets interface to disconnect after 60 seconds of no traffic
Buchanan(config-if)#dialer-group 1	Assigns traffic filtered by dialer-list 1 to this group
Buchanan(config-if)#exit	Returns to global config mode
Buchanan(config)#interface fa0/0	Moves to interface fa 0/0
Buchanan(config-if)#full duplex	Sets duplex to full duplex mode

`Buchanan(config-if)#`**`no shut`**	Turns on interface
`Buchanan(config-if)#`**`interface fa0/0.1`**	Creates a subinterface
`Buchanan(config-subif)#`**`description Management VLAN 1`**	Assigns a local description
`Buchanan(config-subif)#`**`encapsulation dot1q 1 native`**	Enables dot1q encapsulation with VLAN 1 as the native VLAN
`Buchanan(config-subif)#`**`ip add 172.16.1.1 255.255.255.0`**	Assigns IP address
`Buchanan(config-if)#`**`interface fa0/0.10`**	Creates a subinterface
`Buchanan(config-subif)#`**`description Accounting VLAN 10`**	Assigns a local description
`Buchanan(config-subif)#`**`encapsulation dot1q 10`**	Enables dot1q encapsulation on VLAN 10
`Buchanan(config-subif)#`**`ip add 172.16.10.1 255.255.255.0`**	Assigns IP address
`Buchanan(config-if)#`**`interface fa0/0.20`**	Creates a subinterface
`Buchanan(config-subif)#`**`description Sales VLAN 20`**	Assigns a local description
`Buchanan(config-subif)#`**`encapsulation dot1q 20`**	Enables dot1q encapsulation on VLAN 20
`Buchanan(config-subif)#`**`ip add 172.16.20.1 255.255.255.0`**	Assigns IP address
`Buchanan(config-subif)#`**`exit`**	Returns to global config mode
`Buchanan(config)#`**`ip route 0.0.0.0 0.0.0.0 192.168.100.2`**	Defines that all traffic not in local table be routed to address 192.168.100.2 (across Frame Relay link)
`Buchanan(config)#`**`ip route 0.0.0.0 0.0.0.0 192.168.100.6 225`**	Creates a floating static route to send traffic across ISDN Link if Frame Relay network goes down
`Buchanan(config)#`**`ip host Rama 192.168.100.2`**	Sets a local host name resolution to IP address 192.168.100.2
`Buchanan(config)#`**`ip host 2950Core 172.16.1.2`**	Sets a local host name resolution to IP address 172.16.1.2
`Buchanan(config)#`**`ip host 2950-A 172.16.1.3`**	Sets a local host name resolution to IP address 172.16.1.3
`Buchanan(config)#`**`ip host 2950-B 172.16.1.4`**	Sets a local host name resolution to IP address 172.16.1.4

`Buchanan(config)#`**`exit`**	Returns to privileged mode
`Buchanan#`**`copy run start`**	Saves config to NVRAM
Buchanan Core Switch	
`switch>`**`en`**	Enters privileged mode
`switch#`**`config t`**	Enters global config mode
`switch(config)#`**`no ip domain-lookup`**	Turns off DNS queries so that spelling mistakes won't slow you down
`switch(config)#`**`hostname 2950Core`**	Sets hostname
`2950Core(config)#`**`enable secret cisco`**	Sets encrypted secret password
`2950Core(config)#`**`line con 0`**	Enters line console mode
`2950Core(config-line)#`**`logging synchronous`**	Appends commands to new line so that router information won't interrupt
`2950Core(config-line)#`**`login`**	Defines that the user must log in to console before use
`2950Core(config-line)#`**`password rooster`**	Sets password to **rooster**
`2950Core(config-line)#`**`exec-timeout 0 0`**	Console will never log out. Note that this is a security risk in a production environment
`2950Core(config-line)#`**`exit`**	Moves back to global config mode
`2950Core(config)#`**`line aux 0`**	Moves to line auxiliary mode
`2950Core(config-line)#`**`login`**	Defines that the user must log in to auxiliary port before use
`2950Core(config-line)#`**`password crows`**	Sets password to **crows**
`2950Core(config-line)#`**`exit`**	Moves back to global config mode
`2950Core(config)#`**`line vty 0 15`**	Moves to configure all 16 vty ports at same time
`2950Core(config-line)#`**`login`**	Defines that the user must log in to vty port before use
`2950Core(config-line)#`**`password midnight`**	Sets password to **midnight**

`2950Core(config-line)#exit`	Returns to global config mode
`2950Core(config)#ip default-gateway 172.16.1.1`	Sets default gateway
`2950Core(config)#int vlan 1`	Moves to virtual interface VLAN1
`2950Core(config-if)#ip add 172.16.1.2 255.255.255.0`	Sets IP address for switch
`2950Core(config-if)#no shut`	Turns virtual interface on
`2950Core(config-if)#exit`	Back to global config mode
`2950Core(config)#vlan 10`	Creates VLAN 10 and enters VLAN config mode for further definitions
`2950Core(config-vlan)#name Accounting`	Assigns name to VLAN
`2950Core(config-vlan)#exit`	Returns to global config mode
`2950Core(config)#vlan 20`	Creates VLAN 20
`2950Core(config-vlan)#name Sales`	Assigns name to VLAN
`2950Core(config-vlan)#exit`	Returns to global config mode
`2950Core(config)#vtp mode server`	Changes switch to VTP server mode
`2950Core(config)#vtp domain simulation`	Sets name of VTP management domain to **simulation**
`2950Core(config)#interface fa0/1`	Moves to fa 0/1 interface mode
`2950Core(config-if)#desc Trunk link to router`	Creates local description
`2950Core(config-if)#switchport mode trunk`	Turns port to trunking mode
`2950Core(config-if)#interface fa0/24`	Moves to fa 0/24 interface mode
`2950Core(config-if)#desc Trunk link to 2950-B`	Creates local description
`2950Core(config-if)#switchport mode trunk`	Turns port to trunking mode
`2950Core(config-if)#interface fa0/23`	Moves to fa 0/23 interface mode
`2950Core(config-if)#desc Trunk link to 2950-A and member of EtherChannel Group 1`	Creates local description
`2950Core(config-if)#switchport mode trunk`	Turns port to trunking mode
`2950Core(config-if)#channel-group 1 mode on`	Creates an EtherChannel group number 1. All other members of this group must have same number
`2950Core(config-if)#interface fa0/22`	Moves to fa 0/22 interface mode

`2950Core(config-if)#desc Trunk link to` `2950-A and member of EtherChannel Group 1`	Creates local description
`2950Core(config-if)#switchport mode trunk`	Turns port to trunking mode
`2950Core(config-if)#channel-group 1 mode` `on`	Creates an EtherChannel group number 1
`2950Core(config-if)#exit`	Moves back to global config mode
`2950Core(config)#exit`	Returns to privileged mode
`2950Core#spanning-tree vlan 1 root`	Changes this switch to the root switch in VLAN 1
`2950Core#spanning-tree vlan 10 root`	Changes this switch to the root switch in VLAN 10
`2950Core#spanning-tree vlan 20 root`	Changes this switch to the root switch in VLAN 20
`2950Core#copy run start`	Saves config to NVRAM
Buchanan Switch 2950-A	
`switch>en`	Enters privileged mode
`switch#config t`	Enters global config mode
`switch(config)#no ip domain-lookup`	Turns off DNS queries so that spelling mistakes won't slow you down
`switch(config)#hostname 2950-A`	Sets hostname
`2950-A(config)#enable secret cisco`	Sets encrypted secret password
`2950-A(config)#line con 0`	Enters line console mode
`2950-A(config-line)#logging synchronous`	Appends commands to new line so that router information won't interrupt
`2950-A(config-line)#login`	Defines that the user must log in to console before use
`2950-A(config-line)#password rooster`	Sets password to **rooster**
`2950-A(config-line)#exec-timeout 0 0`	Console will never log out. Note that this is a security risk in a production environment
`2950-A(config-line)#exit`	Moves back to global config mode

`2950-A(config)#line aux 0`	Moves to line auxiliary mode
`2950-A(config-line)#login`	Defines that the user must log in to auxiliary port before use
`2950-A(config-line)#password crows`	Sets password to **crows**
`2950-A(config-line)#exit`	Moves back to global config mode
`2950-A(config)#line vty 0 15`	Moves to configure all 16 vty ports at same time
`2950-A(config-line)#login`	Defines that the user must log in to vty port before use
`2950-A(config-line)#password midnight`	Sets password to **midnight**
`2950-A(config-line)#exit`	Returns to global config mode
`2950-A(config)#ip default-gateway 172.16.1.1`	Sets default gateway
`2950-A(config)#int vlan 1`	Moves to virtual interface VLAN1
`2950-A(config-if)#ip add 172.16.1.3 255.255.255.0`	Sets IP address for switch
`2950-A(config-if)#no shut`	Turns virtual interface on
`2950-A(config-if)#exit`	Returns to global config mode
`2950-A(config)#vtp mode client`	Changes switch to VTP client mode. VLAN information will now be copied from 2950Core switch
`2950-A(config)#vtp domain simulation`	Sets name of VTP management domain to **simulation**
`2950-A(config)#int fa0/1`	Moves to interface fa 0/1
`2950-A(config-if)#desc Trunk Link to 2950-B`	Creates local description
`2950-A(config-if)#switchport mode trunk`	Turns port to trunking mode
`2950-A(config-if)#interface fa0/23`	Moves to fa 0/23 interface mode
`2950-A(config-if)#desc Trunk link to 2950Core and member of EtherChannel Group 1`	Creates local description
`2950-A(config-if)#switchport mode trunk`	Turns port to trunking mode
`2950-A(config-if)#channel-group 1 mode on`	Creates an EtherChannel group number 1. All other members of this group must have same number
`2950-A(config-if)#interface fa0/22`	Moves to fa 0/22 interface mode

2950-A(config-if)#**desc Trunk link to 2950Core and member of EtherChannel Group 1**	Creates local description
2950-A(config-if)#**switchport mode trunk**	Turns port to trunking mode
2950-A(config-if)#**channel-group 1 mode on**	Creates an EtherChannel group number 1
2950-A(config-if)#**exit**	Moves back to global config mode
2950-A(config)#**int fa0/6**	Moves to fa 0/6 interface mode
2950-A(config)#**desc Link to VLAN 10 Client Workstation**	Creates local description
2950-A(config-if)#**switchport mode access**	Makes port a VLAN access port
2950-A(config-if)#**switchport access vlan 10**	Statically assigns this port to VLAN 10
2950-A(config-if)#**spanning-tree portfast**	Transitions the port directly to Forwarding state in Spanning Tree Protocol (STP)
2950-A(config)#**int fa0/13**	Moves to fa 0/13 interface mode
2950-A(config)#**desc Link to VLAN 20 Client Workstation**	Creates local description
2950-A(config-if)#**switchport mode access**	Makes port a VLAN access port
2950-A(config-if)#**switchport access vlan 20**	Statically assigns this port to VLAN 20
2950-A(config-if)#**spanning-tree portfast**	Transitions the port directly to Forwarding state in STP
2950-A(config-if)#Ctrl Z	Moves directly to privileged mode
2950-A#**copy run start**	Saves config into NVRAM
Buchanan Switch 2950-B	
switch>**en**	Enters privileged mode
switch#**config t**	Enters global config mode
switch(config)#**no ip domain-lookup**	Turns off DNS queries so that spelling mistakes won't slow you down
switch(config)#**hostname 2950-B**	Sets hostname
2950-B(config)#**enable secret cisco**	Sets encrypted secret password

`2950-B(config)#line con 0`	Enters line console mode
`2950-B(config-line)#logging synchronous`	Appends commands to new line so that router information won't interrupt
`2950-B(config-line)#login`	Defines that the user must log in to console before use
`2950-B(config-line)#password rooster`	Sets password to **rooster**
`2950-B(config-line)#exec-timeout 0 0`	Console will never log out. Note that this is a security risk in a production environment
`2950-B(config-line)#exit`	Moves back to global config mode
`2950-B(config)#line aux 0`	Moves to line auxiliary mode
`2950-B(config-line)#login`	Defines that the user must log in to auxiliary port before use
`2950-B(config-line)#password crows`	Sets password to **crows**
`2950-B(config-line)#exit`	Moves back to global config mode
`2950-B(config)#line vty 0 15`	Moves to configure all 16 vty ports at same time
`2950-B(config-line)#login`	Defines that the user must log in to vty port before use
`2950-B(config-line)#password midnight`	Sets password to **midnight**
`2950-B(config-line)#exit`	Returns to global config mode
`2950-B(config)#ip default-gateway 172.16.1.1`	Sets default gateway
`2950-B(config)#int vlan 1`	Moves to virtual interface VLAN 1
`2950-B(config-if)#ip add 172.16.1.4 255.255.255.0`	Sets IP address for switch
`2950-B(config-if)#no shut`	Turns virtual interface on
`2950-B(config-if)#exit`	Returns to global config mode
`2950-B(config)#vtp mode client`	Changes switch to VTP client mode. VLAN information will now be copied from 2950Core switch
`2950-B(config)#vtp domain simulation`	Sets name of VTP management domain to **simulation**
`2950-B(config)#int fa0/1`	Moves to interface fa 0/1

`2950-B(config-if)#desc Trunk Link to 2950-A`	Creates local description
`2950-B(config-if)#switchport mode trunk`	Turns port to trunking mode
`2950-B(config-if)#interface fa0/24`	Moves to fa 0/23 interface mode
`2950-B(config-if)#desc Trunk link to 2950Core`	Creates local description
`2950-B(config-if)#switchport mode trunk`	Turns port to trunking mode
`2950-B(config-if)#exit`	Moves back to global config mode
`2950-B(config)#int fa0/6`	Moves to fa 0/6 interface mode
`2950-B(config)#desc Link to VLAN 10 Client Workstation`	Creates local description
`2950-B(config-if)#switchport mode access`	Makes port a VLAN access port
`2950-B(config-if)#switchport access vlan 10`	Statically assigns this port to VLAN 10
`2950-B(config-if)#spanning-tree portfast`	Transitions the port directly to Forwarding state in STP
`2950-B(config)#int fa0/13`	Moves to fa 0/13 interface mode
`2950-B(config)#desc Link to VLAN 20 Client Workstation`	Creates local description
`2950-B(config-if)#switchport mode access`	Makes port a VLAN access port
`2950-B(config-if)#switchport access vlan 20`	Statically assigns this port to VLAN 20
`2950-B(config-if)#spanning-tree portfast`	Transitions the port directly to Forwarding state in STP
`2950-B(config-if)#end`	Moves directly to privileged mode
`2950-B#copy run start`	Saves config into NVRAM

Binary/Hex/Decimal Conversion Chart

The following chart lists the three most common number systems used in networking: decimal, hexadecimal, and binary. Some numbers you will remember quite easily, as you use them a lot in your day-to-day activities. For those other numbers, refer to this chart.

Decimal Value	Hexadecimal Value	Binary Value
0	00	0000 0000
1	01	0000 0001
2	02	0000 0010
3	03	0000 0011
4	04	0000 0100
5	05	0000 0101
6	06	0000 0110
7	07	0000 0111
8	08	0000 1000
9	09	0000 1001
10	0A	0000 1010
11	0B	0000 1011
12	0C	0000 1100
13	0D	0000 1101
14	0E	0000 1110
15	0F	0000 1111
16	10	0001 0000
17	11	0001 0001
18	12	0001 0010
19	13	0001 0011
20	14	0001 0100
21	15	0001 0101
22	16	0001 0110
23	17	0001 0111
24	18	0001 1000

continues

Decimal Value	Hexadecimal Value	Binary Value
25	19	0001 1001
26	1A	0001 1010
27	1B	0001 1011
28	1C	0001 1100
29	1D	0001 1101
30	1E	0001 1110
31	1F	0001 1111
32	20	0010 0000
33	21	0010 0001
34	22	0010 0010
35	23	0010 0011
36	24	0010 0100
37	25	0010 0101
38	26	0010 0110
39	27	0010 0111
40	28	0010 1000
41	29	0010 1001
42	2A	0010 1010
43	2B	0010 1011
44	2C	0010 1100
45	2D	0010 1101
46	2E	0010 1110
47	2F	0010 1111
48	30	0011 0000
49	31	0011 0001
50	32	0011 0010
51	33	0011 0011
52	34	0011 0100
53	35	0011 0101
54	36	0011 0110
55	37	0011 0111
56	38	0011 1000

Decimal Value	Hexadecimal Value	Binary Value
57	39	0011 1001
58	3A	0011 1010
59	3B	0011 1011
60	3C	0011 1100
61	3D	0011 1101
62	3E	0011 1110
63	3F	0011 1111
64	40	0100 0000
65	41	0100 0001
66	42	0100 0010
67	43	0100 0011
68	44	0100 0100
69	45	0100 0101
70	46	0100 0110
71	47	0100 0111
72	48	0100 1000
73	49	0100 1001
74	4A	0100 1010
75	4B	0100 1011
76	4C	0100 1100
77	4D	0100 1101
78	4E	0100 1110
79	4F	0100 1111
80	50	0101 0000
81	51	0101 0001
82	52	0101 0010
83	53	0101 0011
84	54	0101 0100
85	55	0101 0101
86	56	0101 0110
87	57	0101 0111
88	58	0101 1000

continues

Decimal Value	Hexadecimal Value	Binary Value
89	59	0101 1001
90	5A	0101 1010
91	5B	0101 1011
92	5C	0101 1100
93	5D	0101 1101
94	5E	0101 1110
95	5F	0101 1111
96	60	0110 0000
97	61	0110 0001
98	62	0110 0010
99	63	0110 0011
100	64	0110 0100
101	65	0110 0101
102	66	0110 0110
103	67	0110 0111
104	68	0110 1000
105	69	0110 1001
106	6A	0110 1010
107	6B	0110 1011
108	6C	0110 1100
109	6D	0110 1101
110	6E	0110 1110
111	6F	0110 1111
112	70	0111 0000
113	71	0111 0001
114	72	0111 0010
115	73	0111 0011
116	74	0111 0100
117	75	0111 0101
118	76	0111 0110
119	77	0111 0111
120	78	0111 1000

Decimal Value	Hexadecimal Value	Binary Value
121	79	0111 1001
122	7A	0111 1010
123	7B	0111 1011
124	7C	0111 1100
125	7D	0111 1101
126	7E	0111 1110
127	7F	0111 1111
128	80	1000 0000
129	81	1000 0001
130	82	1000 0010
131	83	1000 0011
132	84	1000 0100
133	85	1000 0101
134	86	1000 0110
135	87	1000 0111
136	88	1000 1000
137	89	1000 1001
138	8A	1000 1010
139	8B	1000 1011
140	8C	1000 1100
141	8D	1000 1101
142	8E	1000 1110
143	8F	1000 1111
144	90	1001 0000
145	91	1001 0001
146	92	1001 0010
147	93	1001 0011
148	94	1001 0100
149	95	1001 0101
150	96	1001 0110
151	97	1001 0111
152	98	1001 1000

continues

Decimal Value	Hexadecimal Value	Binary Value
153	99	1001 1001
154	9A	1001 1010
155	9B	1001 1011
156	9C	1001 1100
157	9D	1001 1101
158	9E	1001 1110
159	9F	1001 1111
160	A0	1010 0000
161	A1	1010 0001
162	A2	1010 0010
163	A3	1010 0011
164	A4	1010 0100
165	A5	1010 0101
166	A6	1010 0110
167	A7	1010 0111
168	A8	1010 1000
169	A9	1010 1001
170	AA	1010 1010
171	AB	1010 1011
172	AC	1010 1100
173	AD	1010 1101
174	AE	1010 1110
175	AF	1010 1111
176	B0	1011 0000
177	B1	1011 0001
178	B2	1011 0010
179	B3	1011 0011
180	B4	1011 0100
181	B5	1011 0101
182	B6	1011 0110
183	B7	1011 0111
184	B8	1011 1000

Decimal Value	Hexadecimal Value	Binary Value
185	B9	1011 1001
186	BA	1011 1010
187	BB	1011 1011
188	BC	1011 1100
189	BD	1011 1101
190	BE	1011 1110
191	BF	1011 1111
192	C0	1100 0000
193	C1	1100 0001
194	C2	1100 0010
195	C3	1100 0011
196	C4	1100 0100
197	C5	1100 0101
198	C6	1100 0110
199	C7	1100 0111
200	C8	1100 1000
201	C9	1100 1001
202	CA	1100 1010
203	CB	1100 1011
204	CC	1100 1100
205	CD	1100 1101
206	CE	1100 1110
207	CF	1100 1111
208	D0	1101 0000
209	D1	1101 0001
210	D2	1101 0010
211	D3	1101 0011
212	D4	1101 0100
213	D5	1101 0101
214	D6	1101 0110
215	D7	1101 0111
216	D8	1101 1000

continues

Decimal Value	Hexadecimal Value	Binary Value
217	D9	1101 1001
218	DA	1101 1010
219	DB	1101 1011
220	DC	1101 1100
221	DD	1101 1101
222	DE	1101 1110
223	DF	1101 1111
224	E0	1110 0000
225	E1	1110 0001
226	E2	1110 0010
227	E3	1110 0011
228	E4	1110 0100
229	E5	1110 0101
230	E6	1110 0110
231	E7	1110 0111
232	E8	1110 1000
233	E9	1110 1001
234	EA	1110 1010
235	EB	1110 1011
236	EC	1110 1100
237	ED	1110 1101
238	EE	1110 1110
239	EF	1110 1111
240	F0	1111 0000
241	F1	1111 0001
242	F2	1111 0010
243	F3	1111 0011
244	F4	1111 0100
245	F5	1111 0101
246	F6	1111 0110
247	F7	1111 0111
248	F8	1111 1000

Decimal Value	Hexadecimal Value	Binary Value
249	F9	1111 1001
250	FA	1111 1010
251	FB	1111 1011
252	FC	1111 1100
253	FD	1111 1101
254	FE	1111 1110
255	FF	1111 1111

_____

_____

_____

_____

_____

_____

_____

_____

_____

_____

_____

_____

_____

_____

_____

_____

_____

_____

_____

_____